principle

by ⸻wry

12 Winds Publishing, Oklahoma City, Oklahoma

Aikido: Principles of Kata and Randori
By Nick Lowry

Published by:
12 Winds Publishing
4713 Byron Pl
Oklahoma City, OK 73112

©1998 All Rights Reserved. No part of this book may be reproduced by any means, electronic, mechanical, photocopying, recording, or otherwise without written permission from the publisher.

ISBN 1-59113-320-3

Library of Congress Cataloging-in-Publication Data
Lowry, Nick
    Aikido: principles of kata and randori / By Nick Lowry -- 1st ed.
    p.   cm.
Includes bibliographic references and glossary.
ISBN
Library of Congress Catalog Card Number 98-60569
1. Aikido – technical
2. Aikido – practice and theory
3. Aikido – teaching
4. Aikido – philosophy
I.   Title

This book is dedicated to Chuck Caldwell and Karl Geis. These two men have guided me along the path in life and in budo and have inspired me to live my dream.
Thank you, much love, Nick

This book could not have been written without the help, support, and understanding of my loving wife, Louise Rich. I am also indebted to my friends and teachers, Bill Knox, Kitty Sullivan, and Gregory Ables for their editorial assistance, patience, and moral support. I wish to thank especially Glenn Billings (the O sensei of computers and technical proof reader/editor extraordinaire) for his amazing technical support. This work owes a great deal to Sean Ashby whose tireless efforts and remarkable talent illustrate these pages. Thank you Sean.

Finally, I must thank all of my sempai, sensei, and shihan including: Karl Geis, Tsunako Miyake, Henry Copeland, Mac McNease, L. F. Wilkinson, Chuck Caldwell, George Webber, Chris Thygesen, B.G. Smith, Tim Dudley, Jerry Scott, Dennis Doris, Tim Joe, Clif Norgaard, Harry Wright, Rianard Jackson, Ron and Susan Gotlin, Rick Pollard, Ray Williams, John Allen, Ed Bauer, George Hartman, Felix Robles, Paul Legris, Becky Sexton, Al Pezoldt, Kitty Sullivan, Brian Sullivan, Jim Ellison, Will Gable, Charles Cory, and many others, thank you all.

Note on New Edition: Much has changed in our system of Aikido since the publication of this book and though I would like to update it to incorporate the many innovations that have come about, such a revision is not feasible at this time. For a view of the exciting new evolutions in our art, I can only direct your attention to the fine catalog of videotapes and dvds that are available from GW Enterprises whose order form appears at the end of this book. – Nick Lowry

About the Author:

Nick Lowry has been involved in martial arts training most of his life. As a teenager, he studied Musashi's **Book of Five Rings** and the **Tao te Ching** by Lao Tzu while at the same time training in competitive stick fighting. Turning away from the competitive arena, Nick began formal study of budo at Windsong Dojo in Oklahoma City at the age of 18, and he has since earned the ranks: rokudan in Aikido, rokudan in Shindo Muso Ryu Jodo, and godan in Judo. Nick has had the good fortune to train directly under Shihan Karl Geis in aikido, judo and jodo and under Shihan Tsunako Miyake in the study of jodo, goshin jutsu no kata, and koshiki no kata. In addition, he has studied a variety of healing arts including chi gung and masso meridian balancing therapy. Nick has also studied Zen and trained in formal Rinzai zen and Kwan Um (Korean style) zen. Nick holds a M.A. in English, has taught English at the university level, has operated his own dojo, and maintains a variety of artistic interests including painting, stone carving, singing, and poetry. Mr. Lowry continues to train in budo on an almost daily basis and he serves as an assistant instructor to Shihan Charles Caldwell at Windsong Dojo.

About the Illustrator:

Sean Ashby holds a Bachelor of Arts in Graphic Design and Illustration from the University of Central Oklahoma, where he has lived most of his life. He currently holds a nidan rank in aikido, shodan in judo and jodo, and also pursues interests in languages and writing. He lives and works as a designer and illustrator in Oklahoma.

Table of Contents

Warning -- Disclaimer

This book is not intended to be the sole source of information on the art of Aikido for a student and should be used only to compliment, amplify and supplement training under a properly trained, qualified instructor. If you wish to learn aikido, you are urged to seek out a fully qualified instructor. The author and publisher assume no responsibility for any injury, paralysis, or death which may result through the misuse of this text.

Every effort has been made to make this book as complete and accurate as possible. However, there may be mistakes both typographical and in content. Therefore the text should be used only as general guide and not as the ultimate source of information for aikido information. Furthermore it contains information which is current only up to the printing date.

The purpose of this book is to educate and entertain. The author and 12 Winds Publishing shall have neither liability nor responsibility to any person or entity with respect to loss or damage caused, or alleged to be caused, directly or indirectly by the information contained in this book.

If you do not wish to be bound by the above, you may return the book to the publisher for a full refund.

Foreword
from Shihan Charles Caldwell, 7th Dan

It gives me great pleasure to introduce you to my close friend and student, Nick Lowry. Nick is the youngest Shihan that our system of training has yet produced. He is both a skillful exponent of randori and an excellent technician in kata. Beyond this, Nick lives by a life philosophy that I admire greatly. Over the 16 years that Nick has trained with me, his dedication, honesty, loyalty, and friendship have proven invaluable. In truth, he has grown to be like a son to me. Perhaps, I am most proud of the fact that in this time, he has become an exceptional teacher of the art of Aikido in his own right.

In my experience, no book can take the place of a competent teacher; however, books can be of great supplemental value. Nick has written a very fine Aikido book. This book is invaluable to any one interested in the arts and is a **must** for those interested in Karl Geis Ryu or Tomiki Aikido. I have been studying martial arts for 41 years now, and during those years, I've read hundreds of well known and lesser known books related to my chosen arts. Nick's book is written in a way that is easy to follow and understand, and it takes a student from their first day in the dojo right up through their first black belt exam in the Karl Geis Ryu system. It also explores the theories and practice of randori and can serve as a helpful guide in this most difficult area of study. I believe that this is the most complete book of its type I've ever read.

Chuck Caldwell -- Shihan
January, 1998

The Dragon ascends Mt. Fuji, in a
flash but if the snail sets out for Mt.
Fuji, surely he will get there
　　　　-Tesshu

Preface

"Those who know do not speak; those who speak do not know"
Lao Tzu

It is hard to ignore the advice of old Lao Tzu; according to him I should lie low, keep my mouth shut, and avoid criticism. But sometimes, even at the risk of overstepping my ability, I feel it better to try to describe the path I'm on, just on the off chance that it might help somebody out along the way.

I find it ironic that I have undertaken to write a technical aikido book since I, myself, have never been much influenced technically by any aikido book I've ever read. Don't misunderstand me; I've read some great aikido books, and I have learned a lot about ethics, philosophy, and history from these books, but I've never learned much in the way of solid aikido technique from books, and, consequently, I remain doubtful as to the present volume's actual effect.

Putting such doubt aside, I can say that I have tried to write the sort of technical book I would have liked to run across as I was beginning my studies. Hopefully, it will help some of you in your own pursuit of aikido.

When I began my aikido training, I never suspected that I would ever be capable of writing a book like this. I remember many times, during my early years, watching advanced aikidoka and senseis and listening to their technical lessons and thinking that these people are so far beyond me. They're in another world; they're geniuses, and I haven't got a clue! Somehow, with my classmate's and teacher's encouragement, I continued to keep at it, keep training, and keep trying.

As I moved up through my brown belt grades, I began to notice that some advanced students at Aikido clinics were taking notes. When I inquired about this, I found that they were not only taking notes but very careful notes on everything that was being lectured on, whether it be of a technical or philosophical nature. At this time,

I was entering college, and I was quickly becoming convinced of the importance of note taking, so I decided that I, too, would begin to take aikido notes whenever I could in order to keep a record of technical points and lessons. I was further inspired when I learned that Shihan Karl Geis had, himself, made it his practice to take notes when he trained in Japan, where some called him by the nickname, "notebook man."

As the years unrolled and my aikido training continued, I found my life and thought increasingly saturated by aikido, as well as studies in judo and jodo. Through it all, my note taking remained steady, and my progress continued.

Sometime, around my first degree black belt, circumstances compelled me to start my own club and dojo. I quickly learned the tremendous responsibilities and hardships that such an endeavor incurs, and this experience greatly increased my gratitude and respect for my senseis and the amazing job they had done, which had allowed me the opportunity to train and learn.

I also quickly found out the real value of all those notes that I had been taking over the years, for as an isolated teacher, having the ability to draw on the resource of my own aikido upbringing in the form of technical and philosophical lecture notes was a real lifesaver.

As I progressed slowly through the years and dan grades, my note taking intensified, and I included outside research into aikido, through books and films, articles, and conversations with other budoka. I found that, over time, I had accumulated a fairly substantial stockpile of data. I believe now that all of this process was simply a matter of becoming saturated with the subject; I was immersing myself as thoroughly as I could in the subject of aikido training in all of its technical richness.

This aikido book has grown organically out of all these years of note taking, researching and studying. Consequently, I wish to make clear that much of what follows in this book is **not** original. Particularly in my technical descriptions, I find that I resort to descriptions and analogies that have come to me from lessons and notes from many advanced teachers over the years. I find that I cannot, in truth, avoid this, for my very understanding of aikido is caught up with these descriptions of aikido actions and principles that I have adopted from my teachers; they have become my frame of reference. As this book has grown organically out of my notes, it follows that much of my teachers' language and intellectual understanding has found its way into these pages. Please know that I am not trying to steal these lessons and concepts and pass them off as my own. I am merely trying to transmit the best that I have been given in as clear a way as possible. Upon reflection I find that my own contribution in these pages is more as an organizer and conveyor of these lessons through a different media, from the spoken word into the printed, and only secondarily do I contribute my own unique views, lessons, and concepts.

Some Notes on the Use and Abuse of Japanese Terminology

This manual includes some Japanese terminology, but this inclusion is not meant to imply, in any way, that the learning of Japanese words is important to the understanding of the principles or techniques of aikido. As far as the study of aikido is concerned, the **only** reason to learn Japanese terms is for the sake of clarity in communication. If we do not teach our students proper vocabulary, we might in some way be handicapping them in their future training.

For instance, we often find that there are many times in our training that we encounter a certain concept or strategy that we can describe by "painting a verbal picture" of it, but for which the Japanese have coined a simple term. So, we can then adopt the Japanese term as a short hand version of what we are trying to convey, once both parties in the communication share the "verbal picture/ description." This shared understanding allows us to use the vocabulary in a positive, efficient, and constructive way.

Unfortunately, many who make a point to stress formal Japanese vocabulary do so in a destructive way. Most commonly, this abuse takes the form of treating the person who is ignorant of the formal term as some sort of imbecile. A stance of cultural or intellectual elitism takes over whereby the person who is fluent in the vocabulary abuses the person struggling with the vocabulary, simply for the sake of abuse. American tourists who attempt to speak French in France are familiar with this phenomenon. The same thing takes place in some dojos where people get caught up more in "playing Japanese" than in trying to obtain the real heart of the system they are studying.

Of course, we should maintain a deep and abiding appreciation for Japanese culture, but we must also preserve an equally deep and abiding appreciation for our own American culture. In studying the Japanese martial arts, the point must never be to try to act like, sound like, or be like the Japanese, but is instead to obtain a clear understanding of the essential elements of the arts that have been transmitted to us. If learning a few Japanese terms is helpful toward this end, then so be it.

The bottom line remains communication, and like water, communication always finds its own most efficient level. We can see this language use in dojos everyday when we observe students and teachers discussing techniques in terms of "number one, number two, etc." or describing principles in terms of "same hand, same foot; unbendable arm; move your center; eye contact; posture" etc.

We should never scold students for these practices and language habits; for what they are really doing is making these technical and strategic concepts their own on an intellectual level, and they are communicating among themselves in the most easy and efficient way. They are not being "lazy" because it is in the very nature of language that it be adapted and contorted to the ends and purposes of its user; the use of language is always lazy, which is the reason idiom and dialect exist.

However, as a student progresses toward higher rank, we should gently encourage them to get some basic terminology down, if only for the sake of discussing several katas at the same time. For example, it can become confusing when we are discussing "number one," but our partner means "number one of San Kata," and we mean "number one of Ju Nana Hon Kata." Additionally, formal vocabulary is helpful when and if you have the opportunity to communicate with students and teachers from other dojos or systems, for if all you have to fall back on are your dojos special idioms for describing a technique or practice, then it becomes a chore to communicate clearly with someone whose idioms are different.

Thus, the reader should understand that the inclusion of Japanese terminology in this book is meant to serve no other purposes than the purposes of teaching and learning, which are in principle functions of communication.

What Makes Aikido, Aikido?

Aikido is a unique martial arts form with a wide variety of interpretations, and as such, no single explanation of what makes aikido distinctively aikido will suffice. We can, however, approach an answer to this question by examining three of the most common areas of uniqueness: the historical, ethical, and technical aspects of the art.

The history of the art of aikido has been undertaken in numerous works, with various degrees of accuracy. Fortunately, we need not delve too deeply in these murky and sometimes confusing waters in order to gain a perspective on the general history of the art. It is enough to know that aikido is an art that was developed and founded by Morihei Ueshiba (1883-1969), and that it owes a great deal of its form and substance to Daito Ryu Aikijujitsu as taught by Sokaku Takeda (1860-1943). Additionally, one of Ueshiba's top students in aikido's formative years was Kenji Tomiki (1900-1980), a master judo technician, who had trained directly with the founder of judo, Jigoro Kano (1860-1938). Tomiki was very influenced by Kano's rational and analytic approach to the martial arts. Because of Tomiki's educational background, his rational understanding of technical principle, and his exposure to Kano's insight into the principle of ju (gentleness), which had been derived from the Kito Ryu jujitsu school, Tomiki was able to further refine and organize the aikido system of Ueshiba and create his own style, Tomiki Ryu. The distinctiveness of Tomiki's contribution to the art can therefore be seen as the blending of the aiki concepts derived from Daito Ryu and the off balance concepts of ju that stem from old style Kito Ryu jujitsu brought together in a logical and coherent system.

The ethical concepts embodied in the art of aikido also contribute to its uniqueness. Owing largely to the influence of the founder's religious and philosophic bent, we find an extraordinarily high ethical standard and the view that "true budo is love" and that the real purpose of aikido is "to make the whole world one family." Ueshiba clearly believed that aikido principles could transform the

1

world and put and end to violence. This was not a martial art aimed at "beating people," but rather at achieving victory over the self and making peace in the world. Indeed, making harmony out of violence and order out of chaos are the preeminent ethical strategies of aikido, which work in accord with the fundamental values of budo (martial ways) that aim at both the development and refinement of oneself and of one's community. This ethic of budo, which transcends self-interest and seeks to transform the world, was perhaps best described by Jigoro Kano as the spirit of mutual welfare and benefit.

In terms of technical application, with which this book will be most concerned, aikido displays its uniqueness in at least three distinct ways. First and foremost, technical aikido depends upon the use of avoidance (getting off the line of the attack). Shihan Karl Geis tells us that fundamentally aikido is a force avoids force art, whereas in other arts we see force joins with force (judo), or force meets force (karate). In other words, the initial response in aikido, made to any threat or attack, must be to evade the line of the attack and obtain a safe position. Next in uniqueness is aikido's use of off balance in both atemi (striking) and kansetsu (locking) techniques. These concepts of off balance owe a great deal to judo, but in application they are unique and cover a range of interaction that was left out of the formal judo curriculum. Additionally, we can readily find similar techniques of throwing and joint locking in many styles of classical jujitsu, but it is the application of off balance to these techniques that shows the technical distinctiveness of aikido. Finally, we should note the technical uniqueness of aikido in its use of hazumi (power of the momentum of the whole body) over ikioi (impetus of physical strength). Because aikido attempts to work almost entirely from a hazumi mode and thus minimizes the use of strength and muscle, we find that technical aikido applications can be reliably made regardless of size and strength. With proper understanding of hazumi, the small and weak can defend effectively against the large and strong.

These points of uniqueness can all go toward helping answer the question, "what makes aikido, aikido?" But ultimately, you must discover for yourselves the answers to this question. As aikido becomes integrated with your life through the process of training and study, you will develop your own unique interpretation of this art, and you will discover the true heart of aikido that lies beyond history, philosophy, or technique.

Why a Technical Aikido Book?

As was mentioned before, the vast majority of aikido books available for student's reference are largely concerned with the historical and philosophic aspects of the art. This book aims to be different in that the emphasis here is squarely on technical principle. One complication of this aim is that aikido is a multifaceted art and there are many styles of aikido training, each with their own training concepts and vocabulary. Explicitly, the style with which this book is primarily concerned is Fugakukai Aikido, a non-competitive form of Tomiki Aikido, developed and taught by Shihan Karl Geis, but implicitly, with a bit of sensitivity and experimentation, students of other styles should be able to apply these universal technical principles and thereby strengthen their own training and broaden their understanding of pure aikido. In order to do so, all that is required is that the student begin to rationally analyze their own system in light of a few simple technical premises: First, that the lighter and more effortless the technique is, the better; Second, that techniques requiring superior strength, speed, or size are unrealistic in terms of real self-defense; Third, that technical skill is not the product of metaphysical forces or spiritual philosophies, but instead is the product of repetition of efficient physical/mechanical actions; and, Fourth that we should practice our art in such a way so as to insure the cultivation of a real and effective self-defense and not merely be content with aesthetic, philosophic, or spiritual aspects of this art.

Shihan Karl Geis has stated that he finds that the main difference in Aikido styles is not so much in the technical data (after all, good technical principle is good technical principle, no matter what style), but in the manner in which a given system is taught. Some styles stress the philosophical, esoteric, and internal aspects of training early on, while others (this style included) stress the external, pragmatic, and technical side. In either case, we know that the total picture develops over time, and eventually, the student becomes proficient in all areas. Our style's emphasis follows the traditional

4

Tomiki Ryu

budo understanding that "if we diligently develop our waza (technique), our kokoro (minds and hearts) will be improved." In other words, by constantly refining and improving our technical work, we are also constantly refining and improving ourselves, in both obvious and subtle ways. With this understanding, we begin with the focus on the technical side of aikido, not as a rejection of aikido's internal and philosophic aspects but as a means toward growing into them naturally, effortlessly, subconsciously.

As you train in aikido over the years, no doubt you shall meet with, train with, and observe practitioners of many of the different aikido styles. Be assured, you will find profoundly skillful players in all styles; none of them has a monopoly on "good aiki." Of course, all have their strengths and weaknesses, as we all do. Some have greater theoretical understanding, others less. Some have an emphasis on realism, others are strictly concerned with traditionalism, but in any case, all are fine aikidoka. Try not to make divisive criticism for other styles of aikido practice, for we are all branches growing from the same root and in the same rich soil.

With regard to Fugakukai aikido, the following is a list of few of the strong points of our system of training and style of aikido.

1st In Fugakukai Aikido we stress a constant sense of realism in our technique and strive to maintain the highest standard of realistic, fully applicable defensive work possible within the bounds of safety.

2nd To this end we maintain an open ended policy of testing our techniques and principles, and eliminating or altering any that are found to be flawed or ineffective in actual resistive conditions.

3rd We maintain a very high standard of technical understanding based upon actual biomechanical and physical laws.

4th Our system is highly organized into coherent forms that build and develop upon themselves in a logical manner and is thus more accessible to analytic understanding than the more esoteric approaches.

5th We employ a system of toshu randori, not as a competitive form, but as a means of testing our skills and abilities under stress. Randori provides the opportunity to learn valuable skills that are not available in standard kata training.

6th We maintain extraordinary standards of safety in training and stress high ethical values.

The reader should understand that this list is not meant to imply that any other styles are deficient or lacking in these areas. Each style of training has its own unique strengths, and all are valuable. Aikido could not be considered a true and infinite art form if it did not have so many ways to approach, explain, and explore it. We should value our aikido friends from all the styles that we encounter, for no matter whether they be from Tomiki Ryu or Hombu style, Ki Society or Yoseikan, Daito Ryu or Hapkido, they all are wonderful companions on the journey toward the heart of aikido.

Use of this Book

First of all, you should understand that this book of aikido will not teach you aikido. The founder of aikido, Morihei Ueshiba, observed that words and talk cannot encompass aikido. He taught that we can only truly grasp the art through practice. Words can serve as a guide (after all even the founder taught through words) but practice is the key. To learn aikido you need a sensei, a place to train safely, and people to train with. Furthermore, once you have begun training, this book should not be viewed as a replacement in any way, shape, or form for the instruction given by your sensei. It has been written solely for the purpose of **supplementation**. It is the author's hope that this book can add to and augment your aikido training, round out your technical ideas, and broaden your perspectives.

This book is not meant to sow discord or disagreement between any student and his or her sensei, and all students who read this book should adopt a wholly skeptical attitude toward what is herein presented. If a view given in this book differs from your sensei's, you **must** go with your sensei's idea.

The reasons for this are simple. First, the root of your particular aikido training is your sensei. He or she is the only one who can accurately guide your individual progress in the art. Second, aikido is an infinite art form with an equally infinite number of interpretations possible, so to "get stuck" on any interpretation simply because it's in writing is the essence of foolishness. Finally, aikido is an evolving art form that cannot be tied down or captured in the written word. The changes and evolving growth that aikido goes through only take place in actual practice, not through this book or any other. The purpose of this book is to try to pass on some ideas that many students have found useful in their training. Perhaps you will find these ideas useful as well.

Etiquette

Some aikido schools are very heavily oriented toward formal Japanese etiquette. Formal bows, both standing and kneeling, are used, and a strict hierarchy is observed at all times. If you develop these habits of etiquette and hierarchy you will find that you can train at various dojos with the minimum of friction; however, what is most important are the attitudes of respect, harmony, and helpfulness that are implicit in these practices. Sadly, many of the more formal schools have maintained an adherence to the outward form of these practices but have lost the inner spirit. Elitism has replaced respect, and meaningless gestures have replaced real harmony. We must never forget that the practices of etiquette are but an externalization of inner attitudes, and we must never allow empty form to take the place genuine care.

Most commonly, students will first bow when entering the dojo. This bow is basically a moment to recognize and realize both the special nature of the dojo as a place and also to recognize your own reasons and responsibilities upon entering. The dojo is a special place, a transformational environment, and no one who trains long at an aikido dojo remains unchanged, on a variety of levels. This bow upon entry is essentially a recognition of the transformative potential within the place and within yourself. Again, what is most important is not necessarily the outward act of bowing itself but the understanding and attitude that this action represents.

The next bow we most commonly perform occurs while getting on and off the mat. The significance of this bow is much like that of entering into the dojo itself, but more specifically, to bow onto the mat signifies an intent to train, to practice, to grow. This bow is an active realization of the transformative potential. The mat is comparable to an anvil and a forge; stepping on the floor, we enter into the place of tempering, honing, and polishing the self through shugyo (hard practice).

In bowing on the mat, we are bowing to the spirit of shugyo, a truly committed practice, and yet at the same time, we are also

8

bowing to a place of safety and joy. In fact, after a few years training, many people report a feeling of elation or energy by just stepping on the mat. Even in his 80's, Morihei Ueshiba, the founder of aikido, was said to be completely transformed by an energetic and potent force once he got on the mat. On one occasion while desperately ill, he had to be carried to the mat by his students, but once he stepped onto the floor his demeanor and body character changed dramatically into that of an enthusiastic and lively man. He practiced and taught to the very end. For ourselves, we may find that even if we are tired, depressed, or exhausted, once we motivate ourselves to get on the mat, then the effect is palpable. We feel ready to train. We feel happier and energized. Perhaps then we bow in recognition of this amazing feeling when getting on and off the mat.

The next common bow is performed to your training partner. This bow represents a basic attitude of respect on many levels, and is a moment of recognition that we are entrusting our physical well being to one another. Shihan Karl Geis has pointed out that to approach a partner and to **not** bow signifies that a fight is about to commence. The bow is in this way a boundary for defining a training and learning situation as distinct from a conflict situation. In one circumstance, we are joining forces to try to help one another to grow and build toward mastery, in the other we are simply trying to beat our partner and win. Obviously, you will progress far faster by playing under the former rules, and leave winning and beating for the unavoidable conflicts that you meet in the world outside the dojo.

In a very real sense, aikido, as a discipline of study and as a true art form, can only exist in a dojo environment and with this proper understanding, for only in the dojo do we find persons coming together to practice in a spirit of mutual welfare and benefit, helping each other to learn, grow, and take care of one another. The dojo and the tacit understanding of the etiquette make the practice safe -- both in the physical sense of safety afforded us by the mat and psychologically, in that we are agreeing and cooperating with one another in order to train and learn, not fight and kill.

The final most common bow is the class bow, which takes place in a variety of ways. In the author's home dojo, we commonly bow

Bow in Circle, member and hierarchy

in a circle, which is a collective expression of gratitude of students, teachers, and training partners. In the circle, we are also bowing to the circular process of training and teaching; developing better students makes for better teachers, which makes for better students, etc. The circle represents a feedback loop of increasing quality in which all members have a sense of equality. In more formal settings, you might find that a class will line up by ranks and bow to the teacher and possibly toward a picture of the founder of aikido. Some dojos prefer a seated bow (zarei), others prefer a simple standing bow (ritsurei). Bowing in formal lines of rank is representative of respect toward hierarchy and tradition. By bowing toward the founder's picture and/or the sensei, we show respect for the tradition and lineage, to those who have created and refined the art before us. The students bow to honor the debt to the past, the sensei bows back to honor the potential of the future, embodied in the students. In either case these bows signify an expression of gratitude for the art, the teacher, and the student.

Beyond these simple etiquette concepts, we have matters of dojo hierarchy. The hierarchy of the dojo is twofold. First we find the relation between the sensei or teacher (also called a shihan, a leader, if ranked at 6th dan or higher) and the rest of the students, and secondly between sempai (upperclassmen) and kohai (underclassmen).

The sensei or shihan is the teacher or leader of the dojo. He or she is the one responsible for the overall coordination of classes and dissemination of technical information. The sensei is the root resource for the student's development into a genuine aikidoka. The ways that we practice and teach aikido in a particular dojo are based directly upon the sensei's instruction, and the sensei is the ultimate source of evaluation and ranking within his or her dojo.

The second part of the hierarchy is sempai/kohai (higher rank/lower rank), a teaching-learning relationship that is established between partners whenever they get together to train. The sempai guides the practice and helps the kohai. The sempai has more experience with aikido than the kohai, so the relationship is a natural one of gentle guidance and correction. We must always be careful

10

that we don't allow conflict to enter into this relationship by attempting, as kohai, to correct, teach, or criticize our sempai. Sempai is there to help kohai, and sempai has the added responsibility of keeping the practice safe and positive. If kohai does not allow sempai's help and guidance, the learning cannot take place, and practice may become unsafe.

As a teacher or outside observer, it is inadvisable to interrupt or disturb a sempai/kohai interaction except when safety is in question, and even then, if possible, it is best to consult with the sempai privately. Everyone must take responsibility to keep the training safe, regardless of rank or experience.

I. Helpful safety and etiquette guidelines and rules

- Stay focused on the training, be observant of your area, and avoid throwing into the path of other couples' kata, or off the floor. While working on the mat, each aikidoka must be aware of his/her surroundings at all times to avoid potential accidents. As a rule, tori must always look out for uke.
- Remain focused on the lesson or kata demonstration rather than visiting with others. Discussions of safety issues are of particular importance.
- Practice **only** what you have been instructed to practice. Adding something "more advanced" or elements from other arts demonstrates immaturity and unwillingness to receive well planned instruction.
- Refrain from all intoxicants, alcohol or non-prescribed drugs before a lesson.
- If you have a health condition or an injury, advise your sensei and sempai.
- If a technique appears to "fail," slow it down and practice it softer. Speed only leads to frustration, injury, and poor or erroneous technique.
- Aikido is a dangerous art. Every participant must be very careful when applying arm bars, wrist locks, or use of force. We must

11

remain acutely aware of the potential for pain and injury. Pay close attention to all safety issues related to specific techniques - i.e. "cranking," hyper extending, premature release of falling partners, inappropriate acceleration of the throw, etc.

- If sitting on the floor, keep legs folded and pay attention to what is happening around you. If someone falls on your extended legs it will probably injure or break them.
- When learning falls, go at your own pace. Stay within your own personal comfort zone and move on to the more advanced forms only after mastery of the basic forms.
- When learning to roll, spend your first 3-6 months on the safety mats.
- When learning to do elevated break falls (flips), spend the first month on safety mats.
- The most commonly avoidable aikido injuries occur when learning to fall and roll. Keep it slow and safe. Build your falls gradually and they will serve you throughout your life. Falling skills that you develop in the first few months of training are a foundation that will sustain your growth in aikido and make practice come alive. To be a good tori, you must be a good uke, and to be a good uke, you must have good ukemi. If you become injured during this learning period, while building your basic structure, your foundation of ukemi might be flawed and growth may be somewhat stifled. Early injuries can hamper your falling skills and consequently all your aikido skills for years. So stay safe; learn it slow, and learn it right.
- Stay near your partner once they have been thrown in order to protect them from other people falling.
- If you have problems with certain types of ukemi (falling), inform your partner and pat out instead or use safety mats.
- Keep finger and toe nails short so as not to be torn off. Long hair should be put in a ponytail.
- No food or drink is allowed on the mat. Refrain from chewing gum on the mat.
- Refrain from wearing jewelry, perfume or makeup on the mat.

- Make sure your feet and hands are clean before getting on the mat. Keep your body, especially feet, scrupulously clean. Players with dirty feet should not be permitted on the mat.
- If you find blood on the mat, stop and find out who is bleeding. If *you* are bleeding, clean up the mat immediately with peroxide.
- Shoes are not allowed on the mat.

There are no shortcuts
because there is no end.
-- Kyuzo Mifune

Principles of Aikido --Ri

I. Physical Principles

1. Unbendable Arm (Tegatana). The human arm can basically do two things well: it can curl in to pull, and it can straighten out to push. Often in aikido, we use the arm in the pushing position we call unbendable arm. When we engage the arm in this manner, we maintain a slight bend at the elbow (typically, the angle between biceps and forearms is 160° to 170°) and we cock the wrist and fingers back fully to engage us in a push - just as we would use to push a car. By pushing in this way, we are delivering force using the shortest distance between two points, a straight line, and since all arcing motion is minimized, we have the most efficient coverage of distance.

When using unbendable arm, be careful not to lock your elbow straight in an unnaturally hyper extended position. Be careful to keep the fingers up and back - not curled in. The muscles of the arm are basically relaxed, only the muscles of the shoulder, wrist, and fingers are engaged. If tegatana is used consistently, in both tori and uke functions, the timing of attack and defense will become consistent, and since tori will be conditioned to react to the most efficient form of attack, less efficient attacks will automatically become easier to deal with.

15

Unbendable Arm

2. Center (Hara/Itten/Chushin). When we move in aikido, we want to move from the center of our bodies - i.e. our center of gravity (itten), which in upright posture is located in the lower abdomen (hara). Moving from the center means that we should actively feel the beginnings of any stepping action, the weight of our body shifting, at this moment in the direction we are going to travel. The center moves and the feet follow.

Secondly, when we engage our hands to do aikido, we most commonly want them centered, which is to say, inside a space defined by the points of your hips and the tops of your shoulders, extending forward like an imaginary box (chushin) We tend to do most things with our hands in this centered position naturally; to perform actions outside the center often causes strain and imprecision. When our hand is in this centered box, it is in chudan position.

We should note that while most of our hand actions naturally take place in this center position in front of our bodies, there are

16

occasions when our hands will leave this central box. We see this in the katas when the hand and arm move to a low side position in gedan-ate, or when the hand rises above shoulder height (jodan gamae) to push in oshi-taoshi, ude-gaeshi, kote-hineri, shiho-nage, and tenkai kote-hineri.

These actions where the hand leaves the center are natural and useful, but only so long as the energy transmitted through these hand and arm positions continues to come from the movement of the center (hara), the total body action, and not from the shoulder or arm itself.

In addition, the centering concept of chushin can be expanded to include the "center line," which is the central axis for a given mass. The center line for a human body is an imaginary line that divides the body or body part into equal and symmetrical halves. Almost all attacks and techniques are employed against the center line of the body, thus using maximum effect with minimum effort.

So, we can see then that center relates in three basic ways. First, it relates to the window of efficient placement of the arms and hands in front of the center of the body. Secondly, center relates to the center of gravity in the lower half the abdomen where the force of the push is generated in motion. To deliver force without altering the position of the center of gravity is ineffective and self-limiting. Third, in manipulating the center line we find maximum effectiveness. These principles of center are the keys to the model of efficient motion.

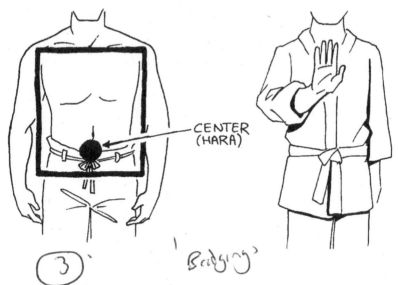

CENTER
(HARA)

(3)

Bridging

3. Same Hand and Foot (Namba) When we use our movement to deliver energy to our partner in aikido we try to do it in the most efficient biomechanical way. If we are pushing or pulling, this means we try to ensure that we are bridging our body weight from the opposite leg to the hand that is doing the work. This means that if we push with our right hand, our right leg will be forward and our body weight will be bridged from our left foot to our right hand. The force of the push is transferred from the back leg to the forward hand. In essence, we are using our hand like a leg, and we are "stepping" onto a vertical surface just as you would lean against a wall for support.

Same hand and foot position gives us postural stability and the ability to deliver the maximum load of body weight over the maximum distance to travel in a single step to the target. In addition, this delivery of energy takes place over the entire length of the step; anywhere that you make contact with your opponent within the space of the step will deliver the energy that you generate. Thus, you have a huge window for effectiveness as compared to strikes, kicks, or punches that have only a small window of effectiveness.

In pulling, the action is reversed. The hand that is pulling is paired to the same side leg stepping back. The pull comes from the center dropping in a step; the arm stays relaxed, and energy is transmitted efficiently. In either pushing or pulling, the hand and foot on the same side of the body are engaged.

Same hand same foot

4. Eye Contact (Metsuke). When we engage in aikido we train to look our partners in the eyes, but eye contact is more difficult than it seems since we are taught from childhood that it is normally rude or inappropriate to look intently into someone's eyes. However, if we

focus on eyes
for distance

train consistently in this way, it yields a number of good results. By learning to make eye contact without sending any signals with our eyes, our eyes become highly acute receivers of data and information. By maintaining eye contact, we quickly learn to subconsciously read our partner's intention and direction of movement. Additionally, with eye contact at the correct distance, called ma-ai, we maintain a peripheral view of our partner's entire body, head to toe.

By keeping the eyes and head aligned with the torso, eye contact automatically centers our body toward our partner's center line. Additionally, we use our eyes as a subconscious trigger for intuitively gauging ma-ai distance. By consistently focusing on a given object (i.e. your partner's eyes), the focal point of the two eyes form a parallax (the convergence of the two lines of sight on a given point) - when the parallax reaches the optimum angle (at ma-ai) you train to always react with defensive reflex. Subconsciously, we sense the parallax of our eyes when our partner reaches the given distance and it is thus through the practice of eye contact that we develop our sense of ma-ai.

Eye contact is perhaps the most difficult aikido principle to maintain, but stick with it. As you progress in aikido training, eye contact will change after a number of years, and you will develop what is called enzen no metsuke "looking at the distant mountains," a defocused gaze that allows your subconscious automatic responses to become primary. Do not try to make this transition happen or you may cause defects to slip into your practice. The defocused gaze will come on its own; don't be premature, you must spend the requisite years using eye to eye contact consistently for the defocused gaze to develop properly into the subconscious form.

By using eye contact, you build a reflexive perceptive mechanism for judging the angle, distance, and timing of an attack. This mechanism becomes consistent so that you can build a reliable subconscious trigger for reaction. This trigger of reaction is necessary for response in evasion and in alignment of your center with the attacker's center.

5. Posture (Shizen-hon-tai). Maintaining good posture is also a difficult aikido principle for many people. Taller men have an especially difficult time keeping their head in good alignment. Proper posture for aikido basically consists of putting your weight on the balls of your feet so that your heels are barely touching the floor. Professor Tomiki said that your heels should be up just enough that a single sheet of rice paper could pass beneath them. Your weight is evenly distributed 50/50 on both feet. Your knees are slightly bent; hips are slightly forward; chest is out; head is up, and arms are relaxed at your sides, hanging loose. You should feel that from the top of your head down to your tail bone is one solid unit. The head should not turn or duck. Shoulders stay aligned with hips, and upper body is centered over your hips. Chest and shoulders are pulled back in a feeling of powerful openness.

This postural alignment allows you to remain in a state of readiness to move with the most efficient framework possible. Your weight is supported by the muscles of the legs that are working to hold you up in readiness for action. If you straighten your knees and put weight flat on your feet, you are in a resting posture and are unable to immediately respond with movement in certain directions. Secondly, your upper body is kept from tilting forward or back so that the force of gravity is minimized over your structural support (feet, legs, hips). Obviously, the more the upper body is tilted out of center, the more work you must do to support yourself. Good posture is essential for clean and efficient movement and optimal responsiveness. Professor Tomiki, the founder of Tomiki Ryu Aikido, called this the principle of "natural body" (shizen no ri), and he described it as an unrestricted posture from which it is possible to attack and defend by adapting to any kind of assault. Furthermore, Tomiki pointed out that this posture is a form of mugame (no stance), which had long been a secret principle of kenjutsu (swordsmanship); whereby, we are able to respond to attacks without assuming any preparatory stance. This concept of mugame is also closely linked to mushin (no mind), a completely spontaneous and automatically reactive mind set that is unhindered by planning or plotting out what you must do next. A natural posture and a natural mind are essential aikido principles.

From this we should note that when we engage in a push, we keep our aikido posture constant. Since a push is capable of delivering far more energy than a strike or punch and does so over a much greater distance (that is, the window of the delivery of a push corresponds to the length of the step, not to the rotation of the hips as in a strike), then the posture of the body should be a pushing posture, which emphasizes the relation of the hips and back to the arm from an upright position. Head is up; chest, abdomen, and hips forward, knees slightly bent; weight is evenly distributed on the balls of the feet. Even while pushing, we should not bend forward at the hips, for this variation of the fundamental posture will cause a distortion of balance and limit our ability to move freely.

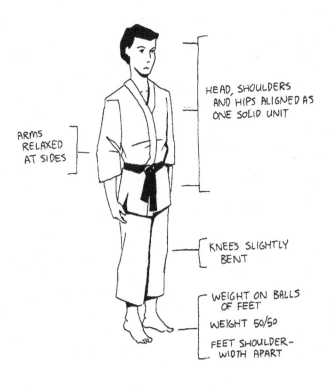

HEAD, SHOULDERS
AND HIPS ALIGNED AS
ONE SOLID UNIT

ARMS
RELAXED
AT SIDES

KNEES SLIGHTLY
BENT

WEIGHT ON BALLS
OF FEET

WEIGHT 50/50

FEET SHOULDER-
WIDTH APART

6. Move Off the Line of Attack (Taisabaki). Evasion is an essential component of aikido techniques and is the defining quality of the art. As was noted previously, Shihan Karl Geis has explained that martial arts are essentially defined by their initial automatic response to attack. Hard style arts use a force meets force approach such as an initial response of a block. Grappling arts, such as judo, use a joining force response in which our initial response is to join our center to the attacker's center and control it. In aikido, the initial reaction to attack is to avoid the force of the attack. We refer to this as moving off the line of the attack. Tomiki discussed this evasive response as an application of ju no ri, the principle of gentleness, and described it as avoiding or accepting an attack with body movement.

It is important that when we move off the line we do so by moving our center (our whole body) in an efficient manner (i.e. the center drops in the direction of the step - feet follow the center's movement) and that both feet move to complete the action. The distance of off -line movements is relative and may be as much or little as several feet, a few centimeters, or only a pivoting of the hips and feet.

The line of the attack is defined by the direction of the attacker's center moving through space toward our center. The angle of hands, feet, or weapons employed in the attack are considered secondary lines of attack, but the primary line of attack is always defined by the direction of movement of the attacker's center.

For efficient evasions, we must consider unsoku (footwork) and we must consider the lines down which our feet naturally travel. We begin by assuming that we are moving forward, since most of our time is spent moving this direction. But when stepping forward, we do not travel in as straight a line as we appear. The angle of movement of our individual feet is hardly ever on the line down which we travel; certainly, we know that no one walks normally as if on a tight rope (feet exactly on the line of travel). We actually move off in the direction that our toes are pointing, right then left, alternately, in order to go forward. This normal walking, alternating feet, is called ayumi ashi. If viewed from above, this movement of the body creates a slight wave line as the body moves forward. If this process is interrupted, as happens in an evasion step, then we continue down the line of the forward foot, which is already off the line of attack, and we let the back foot follow (tsugi ashi or following foot step). By not counteracting the forward foot waver and instead letting the rear foot follow, a deviance off the original line of travel occurs. This type of evasion is the most natural evasion possible since it does not require preparation or anticipation to initiate it. Only one transition of motion need be made to effect this evasion (from alternating foot to following foot), The advantage of this form of evasion is that in this form there are no loading or turning movements implied here as there are in other evasive vectors (such as moving backwards, circularly, or side to side). These other vectors of evasion are also effective; however, they are more technically complex and require earlier recognition time in order to initiate them. For instance, in order to evade by stepping backwards we would need to stop any forward momentum that we might have and then reverse ourselves. This extra movement takes extra time and requires that we anticipate the attack earlier. Such evasion is practical only if one happens to be standing still, with weight even on both feet, at the moment of engagement; otherwise it stands a strong chance of failure.

Off the line of attack

7. Distance (Ma-ai). Ma-ai is the distance or the point in space and time between you and your partner where you must begin to act or evade; consequently, developing a sense ma-ai is the beginning developing a sense of timing. Ma-ai is arguably the most important aikido principle, for without a consistent and reliable sense of ma-ai, all of the other principles become useless. Ma-ai is technically

26

defined as the distance at which, while looking at our partner's eyes, we can also peripherally just see his feet. For simplicity's sake, ma-ai is usually defined as "two arms length with hands raised distance." We measure off our ma-ai in practice before each kata in order to reinforce proper distance and reaction in time. If your evasion is late and ma-ai has been violated, then your chances of being struck go up substantially. If uke is allowed to launch an attack from within ma-ai, then evasion becomes difficult, if not impossible. Conversely, if you evade too early, while uke is still outside of ma-ai, then uke will be able to adjust and track your evasion. Thus, ma-ai is not only your critical safe distance, but also the critical moment of commitment in any legitimate attack. Once uke commits the attack at ma-ai, his chances of adjusting or tracking your evasion go down considerably. For uke, ma-ai is a point of no return.

Ma-ai also varies according to special conditions that are addressed in the higher katas, for instance, in situations where you are seated and uke is standing, or when uke is armed with a weapon, or is using variable or excessive speed. Another special use of ma-ai is to use a delayed evasion, sometimes called "letting them into ma-ai," as in the Big 10.

Ma-ai

8. Body Drop and Body Rise (Ue-Shita). This principle relates to how our bodies move when we take a step. In each given foot cycle (movement of both feet), there is a body rise (ue) and body drop (shita) as the weight of the body is transferred from one foot to the other. As the center of gravity goes through this up/down cycle, the top of the cycle manifests a relative lightness and the bottom of the cycle, a relative heaviness; in other words, half the time your body is pushing its own weight up into the air, and half of the time it is falling to the earth. In the falling phase of the cycle, you have the maximum capacity to deliver energy (the energy of body weight multiplied by momentum that gravity produces); moreover, in the dropping phase, the musculature of the body is naturally in the process of pushing to catch the falling weight of your own body. In body rise, the foot continues pushing until it rises, weightless, off the ground, and in this phase, the delivery of energy is diminished at the point of equilibrium that occurs at the peak of body rise. Learning to recognize and feel this rising and falling cycle both in ourselves and in our partners allows us to throw and control with a minimum of force.

Your goal is to go through an entire class and feel Nothing —no pressure, no exertion at all.
-Karl Geis

II. Conceptual Principles

We can refer to kuzushi, tsukuri and kake as "conceptual" principles because they exist only in an abstract way, for it is only within the flow of the relationship between tori and uke that we can find them. Tori and uke are themselves abstractions that have been found useful in delineating the flow of interaction between partners in training; tori is the role of someone applying a technique, and uke is the role of someone receiving the technique. In kata, these roles are well defined and reinforced, but in randori the roles are much more fluid and interchangeable.

1. Kuzushi (balance breaking). Kuzushi is any movement that disturbs uke's intention, balance, posture, momentum, line of attack, or distribution of weight. Ideally, kuzushi effects a state of dis-balance in such a way as to produce a state of dependent disequalibrium in which uke actually comes to depend on tori for stability and reference. By redirecting the line of force of uke's attack, be it by several feet or by a few inches, tori causes a disruption in time, balance, and intention, which must be compensated before any secondary attack may be launched. If applied with great subtlety and sensitivity to uke's compensatory reactions, various waza (techniques) can be completed by resorting to successive applications of kuzushi, in other words, by continuously disturbing uke's line of attack and recovery, uke's efforts will consistently degenerate until uke can no longer maintain architectural stability. In a more limited sense, kuzushi is considered to be the initial phase of the technique, wherein tori breaks uke's balance.

2. Tsukuri (fitting). Tsukuri is any move that accommodates or fits in with uke's intention, posture, momentum, or line of attack. By manipulating the timing and distance of reaction with great sensitivity, tori can harmonize completely with uke's actions, enter uke's weak zones and maintain a consistent relationship to uke in such a way as to seem impossible to feel or touch. Tsukuri is accomplished through continuously responding to uke's attacks and recoveries by evading and moving in synchronicity with uke. This principle is ideally exemplified by tori's not putting any additional energy into the physical system and staying in perfect rhythm with uke. In this way, the inertia of uke's attacks and recovery steps come to create small inefficiencies that are constantly building up as he continues to attack. Tsukuri has the effect of causing uke to feel very little of tori; in the best case, to feel nothing, so that uke's attacks generate energy that he himself must absorb. Tsukuri has a very light and effortless feel to it, and it allows uke to experience minute delays in recovery that eventually cause disequalibrium. In a more limited context, tsukuri is the second phase of a technique in which tori responds to uke's attempt to recover balance.

3. Kake (termination). Kake is any movement that terminates uke's intention and line of attack to such a degree that uke can no longer remain in a viable offensive position. Uke can no longer recover and attack. Kake is the concluding action of a throw or lock in which tori exerts force upon a weakness in uke's position, balance, or posture. Typically, kake is conceived of as a active throw or lock that exploits uke's vulnerability in a particular direction. Though kake is a use of force, if it is applied correctly, in the proper time and position, kake should not feel strenuous or excessive. Thus, kake is an application of strength to weakness, not strength to strength.

III. Application of Conceptual Principles

As mentioned before, each of these principles may be manifested in a given aikido technique as distinct components, but also, these principles can be emphasized and repeated within a given technique. Because they all produce similar, disturbing effects in uke, they are somewhat interchangeable, so that conceptually, a technique can be accomplished through successive applications of kuzushi alone, tsukuri alone, or kake alone. Normally, they occur in combinations that complement one another. Especially in the case of tsukuri, which is the most passive of the three, it would be unlikely that a given, specified throw or lock could be accomplished through only fitting in. In this case, a throw or lock would occur, but it would not necessarily be what tori had intended, since by definition tori would not add energy to the dynamic system to effect change, and uke's predicament and ukemi become entirely determined by the naturally degenerative process, independent of tori's control, and dependent upon the speed and angle of uke's recovery being matched perfectly by tori's strategic use of tsukuri.

In a similar sense, a throw or lock executed with only kuzushi will also depend primarily on uke's actions of attack and recovery, but here tori does intentionally re-direct uke into a specified postural distortion that limits the set of possible recovery steps and actions considerably; thus, more control is assumed by tori over the outcome.

In kake, tori exploits a weakness in uke, thereby determining, to the greatest degree, the throw or lock that he intends. To be sure, uke's speed, rhythm, inertia, and direction of recovery are significant in the application of kake, but the overwhelming control of the technique's execution is in tori's hands. In a different sense, these three principle concepts can be conceived of as differing applications of timing. When tori's and uke's timing is synchronous, kuzushi is implemented; when tori is slightly ahead of uke, kake is the result; and when tori is slightly behind in time (i.e. responding to uke), we have tsukuri. And since time and distance are relative to one another, we can see that these variables will cause different outcomes in a given technique.

For instance, in the technique, shomen-ate, when time and distance are equal, we find that uke is thrown down a line that is roughly perpendicular to his original line of force. This type of shomen ate is a normal manifestation of a kuzushi application and is the standard kata form:

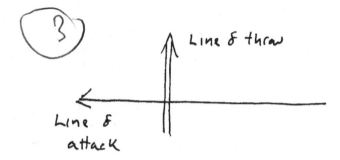

But when tori takes the initiative and is slightly ahead of uke in time and distance, uke is actually interrupted in a weakness of body rise and is thrown back down the original line of attack. This line is typical of a kake application:

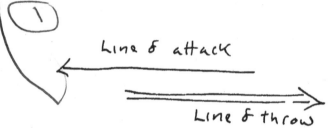

Finally, when tori responds to uke's attack slightly late in time, he will find himself in a position similar to uke's, and the throw will take place down the same line as the attack, as a tsukuri application:

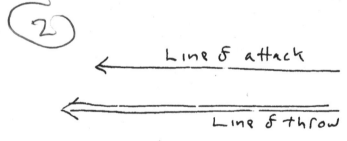

In each case, tori makes an identical response (shomen-ate), but because of the differences in time, the relative position between tori and uke alters and the throw unfolds differently.

Of course these examples are simplifications; in actuality, we make our transitions between these three modes of action while remaining largely unaware of them. Furthermore, a case can be made that in a perfect execution of technique, these elements should take place simultaneously, rather than sequentially; kuzushi, tsukuri, and kake, all at once. Such application could be considered an example of kime (unified decisive action). Alternatively, our consideration of these principles may also lead us to view them as matters of initiative (sen). The order in which the conceptual principles are applied in a given encounter all relate to sen, for it is with sen that we find if we are functioning in a manner that is proactive (sen-sen no sen), simultaneously active (sen), or reactive (ato no sen).

Students Notes:

Preparing the Body

I. Stretching

At the beginning of class, we generally go through a series of stretches and warm up exercises. It is important to stretch slowly into your own comfort zone and **without bouncing**. Bouncing stretches can actually cause muscle contractions and tears. Slow, gentle, concentrated stretching is best. The amount of time the stretch is held varies from teacher to teacher. Some prefer a long count of up to 20 or more, others prefer 3 to 5 seconds, repeating the stretch several times. Both ways are safe and effective.

To enter into proper stretching mode, go to the limit of your comfortable range of motion and as you exhale, extend the stretch gently to mild discomfort. Never stretch to acute pain, and be particularly careful when stretching injured parts of the body. If you properly stretch with the correct concentration, you will likely break a light sweat about midway through the routine, a good indication that you are doing it right.

The position of the head is important in your stretches. Try to keep your head up and in alignment with your spine throughout the stretch. Doing so will concentrate the stretch on the proper body area and minimize muscle tears.

The purpose of these stretches is threefold. First, stretching allows you the opportunity to become aware of any minor injuries or problem areas that you may have overlooked, so that you can take proper precautions with these areas during training. Secondly, stretching warms up the primary muscle groups and increases circulation in order to prepare the body for athletic movement. Thirdly, stretching increases flexibility of the joints, tendons, ligaments and large muscle groups to minimize injury and create better posture and bodily control.

The stretching routine that we usually practice is some variation of the following:

1. Seated with feet apart - twist around and touch hands to the floor behind your back - keep head up.

2. Seated with feet apart - reach down to one side and grasp foot with both hands - head up. Then repeat on opposite side.

3. Seated with feet apart - stretch down and grasp both feet - head up.

4. Seated with one leg bent in to inner thigh - stretch down to straight leg with hands on shoulders or holding the foot - head up. Repeat on opposite side.

5. Seated with feet together sole to sole "butterfly" - stretch down with hands on shoulders - head up.

6. Seated in butterfly (as in previous movement) - grasp ankles or feet and pull in.

7. Seated with legs extended together, toes pointed away - stretch down with hands on shoulders - head up.

8. Seated with legs extended together, toes curled in - stretch down with hands on shoulder -head up.

9. Seated with legs extended together - grasp soles/toes with both hands and lift heels.

10. Seated with one leg bent - hold inner arch of the foot - elevate foot and straighten leg - You may put the opposite hand on knee for support. Repeat on opposite side.

11. Kneeling - grasp opposite foot with hand from behind - stretch forward for the thigh stretch -touch foot to buttocks for the knee flex. Repeat on opposite side.

12. On hands and feet with hips up - stretch calf muscles alternating, then walk it out.

13. Wrist stretches

   a) Kote gaeshi - hand turned in.

b) Kote hineri - hand turned out and under.

c) Kote mawashi - hand turned out and up.

14. Shake out hands and stretch and flex fingers. The same may be done with ankles and toes. If a neck stretch is done, only flex in one direction at a time - no circular movements.

II. Ukemi: The Art of Receiving the Attack

Ukemi practice is the next part of the warm-ups and consists of a number of athletic ways to fall and dissipate the force of a fall safely. Learning to fall correctly is a fundamental skill that will foster your overall technical growth. The quality of your falling skill will directly impact the quality of your attacks as uke – in fact ukemi literally means "what uke does" and so in some sense ukemi and attacking are already understood to be linked. Since your ability as uke will deeply effect your understanding of tori, the skills of ukemi take on even more significance. We develop our sense of off balance by being in off balance, and our sense of how to throw, by being thrown. More than just being simple ways to keep from getting injured in a fall, these skills form a foundation for the entire art. These falling forms involve a few key elements that are consistent throughout.

Keys to Falling:

1. In order to prevent head impact, keep your head up off the mat with your chin tucked in. When you begin to learn this, your neck may be a little sore from using muscles that you don't normally use.
2. Slap with your palms down, and keep your arms relaxed and rounded. Don't hyper extend your elbow. Slap as your shoulder blades touch the mat, with your arms at a comfortable angle from your shoulders; do not slap too high. The arm position is closer to the thigh than the shoulder.
3. Never reach for the ground as you begin to fall. This results in broken arms, wrists, and shoulders.
4. Breath out as you slap. Your lungs must be deflating as you fall, or you can have your breath knocked out and bounce like an inflated ball.
5. Stay rounded in your back as you fall so that your body rolls smoothly in the plane of the fall.

6. Relax your abdomen with your exhalation so that you don't bounce and have to take more than one impact.

The Basic Falling Routine is as follows:

Ushiro Ukemi or Koho Ukemi (back falls)

1. Lying down - chin tucked - slap (8 times).
2. Sitting - roll back - chin tucked - slap (8 times).
3. Squatting - roll back - chin tucked - slap (8 times). Do not do squatting position if you have knee problems.
4. Standing - rise on the balls of your feet - extend hands to the front - bend knees and gently roll back - chin tucked - slap (8 times).

Yoko Ukemi (side falls)

5. Squatting side fall (do not do if you have knee problems). Slide foot across in front of body - simultaneously reach across in same direction - roll up extended leg and side - slap keeping chin tucked (8 times).

6. Standing side fall. Slide foot across front of body - simultaneously bring arm across in same direction as foot - bend support leg and roll up extended leg and side - slap keeping chin tucked (8 times).

7. Side Slaps. Lying on the floor on your side, keep feet apart and turned into full slap position - rock up to the shoulder blades - rotate and come down to other side - coordinate the slap of the feet and hand - do not allow legs to cross - keep knees apart, as if a barrel was between them (8 to 20 times).

Mae Ukemi (front falls)

8. Front Falls. From a kneeling position tip forward landing squarely on forearms and hands palm down.

   From standing same as above.

   Advanced form   from standing reach down with one hand and kick feet out from beneath you as you lower yourself down on your support hand.

Rolling Breakfalls   Zempo Kaiten Ukemi

Never be in a hurry to advance into rolling breakfalls. You must always stay in your comfort zone and be very cautious about any hard impact on the shoulder or hip. When learning these falling skills, spend your first several weeks or months on the safety mat, if possible. If you develop any problem with falls, then return to the safety mat until the problem is resolved.

First Form: We begin with a half kneeling leg out to the side position, make sure that the leg that is outstretched is straight and toes are pointed forward - place the hand on the kneeling side beneath you and reach as far back as possible between the legs with palm down - as you reach back allow your shoulder and head to rest on the floor - you can brace with your free hand in front - then push off into a forward roll.

The first form is the safest form of roll. When done properly it eliminates all impact on the shoulder and will allow the internal gyroscope in your inner ear to get acquainted with the angle of a proper rolling fall. This form is especially important if you do not have a safety mat available to learn on.

Second Form: Is a regular kneeling form - head down - chin tucked - arms form a circle near the front foot - palms down - keep body tucked in a ball as you push off with back leg into a roll - slap into a side slap position.

Third Form: Standing roll. Place feet in a 90° angle like a letter L - place hands by front foot - tuck chin - lift back leg up until gravity tips you forward into a fall - rolling diagonally across the back - slap in a side slap position.

Fourth Form: Standing - place feet in a 90° angle - as you put hands down to position, raise back leg - body like a teeter totter - until gravity tips you forward - roll and side slap.

Fifth Form: Once you have demonstrated that you can consistently land safely in the side slap position, you can begin to come up to a standing position. To begin this process, start out in your slap position on the ground - bend forward and down with your trunk, simultaneously pushing with your hands together and walk yourself up on your hands. You will rotate around the axis of the hands and top leg (keep the bottom leg relaxed), and as you push on this axis you will be turned and looking back in the direction you fell from as you rise. By keeping the body curled forward in the roll, you keep your center of gravity rolling up over your legs, and the power of the momentum of the fall is used efficiently to return to standing.

Keep the legs basically straight with some flex at the knees as you push yourself upright. Be careful not to bend the knees and roll up on them. *Coming up on the bent knee is a common practice in many schools and in many styles; however, the prevalence of this form is unfortunate since this antiquated form can lead to injuries.*

The following advanced ukemi should not be attempted without previous mastery of 1st - 5th forms:

Sixth Form: Standing side fall into roll. Start with feet square - as you begin to tip over sideways, allow your weight to come up on the ball of your support leg - turn into a pivot on the foot as you go into a forward roll.

Seventh Form: Backward turn into roll. Start with feet square - lift one foot up in front as high as it will go - put weight onto ball of foot of support leg pivoting 180° - forward roll.

Eighth Form: Hop, skip and roll. Vary elevation, forward distance, and momentum of roll. Make changes incrementally, and keep it safe.

Ninth Form: Opposite hand and foot roll.

Tenth Form: No arms roll.

Eleventh Form: (Tobu Ukemi) Metatarsal kick into elevated breakfall or forward flip.

Common Problems to Look Out For in Rolling Breakfalls

1. Turning the head as you fall to look at the ground. When the head is turned, the shoulder and hip become vulnerable because you are turning in two planes at the same time.

2. Jumping into the roll. This occurs because it is difficult to let go of control and let gravity tip you over into the fall. Jumping is a form of controlling the fall that may make the fall more dangerous because by jumping we are adding energy to the fall.

3. Letting the front foot turn in as the fall begins. This alters the angle of the hips and shoulder and acts like a less severe form of turning the head.

4. Turning on the heel instead of the ball of the foot in turning falls.

5. Holding the breath during the fall.

6. Letting the back knee fold under as you come back up. This endangers the knee, shin, and ankle if the fall unexpectedly turns into a flip. This position also makes one vulnerable to the heel strike from the top leg as it descends. People falling in this way have been known to literally break their own legs.

Student Notes:

Kata

I. Tegatana no Kata (hand/arm sword form)-- The Walking Kata

1. Shomen Ashi--forward step
2. Waki Ashi--side to side step
3. Tenkan Ashi--pivot step
4. Shomen Te Gatana--forward push
5. Uchi Mawashi--inside sweep
6. Soto Mawashi--outside sweep
7. Uchi Soto Gaeshi--inside/outside reversal
8. Uchi Mawashi Gaeshi--inside sweep reversal
9. Soto Mawashi Gaeshi--outside sweep reversal
10. Ude Goshi Gaeshi--arm hip reversal
11. O Mawashi--major sweep
12. Yoko O Mawashi--side major sweep

Tegatana no Kata is the most important kata for building a sound structure for all aikido movements. Generally speaking, the walk contains all the fundamental movements that will be applied in later katas and randori. By learning to coordinate the actions of the center, hands, and feet in this distilled and purified form, you will have all the components in place for your aikido practice. Shihan Karl Geis has called the walk the fundamental alphabet and vocabulary out of which the "language" of aikido is constructed. From this simple set of rules and basic elements, the virtually infinite possibilities of aikido become manifest. The walking kata itself builds from the simplest movements toward the more complex, and it is an excellent kata for solitary study. By simply attempting to apply all the aikido principles consistently, you can find many years worth of work in this single kata. For many years, the author practiced this kata daily on his own; Shihan Caldwell made it his practice to do the walk for up to an hour a day for several years, and Shihan Karl Geis once said that the real secret to his advanced randori skill was that he could walk more efficiently than the other advanced players.

To refine our study, we should practice this kata by constantly paring it down to its most simple form. Try to constantly eliminate unnecessary movements and adjustments. Become acutely aware of the weight distribution on your feet. Learn to control even the smallest of bodily actions. Focus your eyes on a single point at eye level in the distance. Concentrate on the turning actions of the hand, hips, and feet. Keep unbendable arm. Let the center fall into each step. Move your center where you want it, and let the feet line up under it. Try to stay completely level. Learn to completely open and close your hips. Begin and end each step with the weight even on both feet. Keep your weight off your heels. Explore how large you can make each action and how small. Concentrate on breathing actions and how they relate to pushing actions. Try the kata as fast as possible and as slow. When practicing with the class, try to move in perfect synchronicity in time with the person leading the count. Try to end on the exact spot you began.

These are only a few of the points to concentrate on and explore when practicing the walking kata, and over time, you will find just as many for yourself as you study this great kata. Above all, don't get discouraged; Shihan Caldwell once asked Shihan Tsunako Miyake, who was instrumental in creating the kata, how long it took her to perfect the walking kata, and she replied that she didn't know because she had only been doing it for thirty years! With that as an learning example, we can rest assured that we will all have alot of work on this "basic" kata ahead of us.

Technical notes on Tegatana no kata
* Points to keep in mind with the walking kata *
When a primary hand action is taking place, the secondary hand should engage also but on the plane of the hips as an action to protect the groin. This secondary action helps to establish a balanced physiological symmetry as the wrist and hand action mirror the larger, primary action.

With all the turning actions of the feet, don't allow the second foot to splay out behind, but rather bring the secondary foot back to shoulder width, nearly square, and weight 50/50 on both feet.

1. Shomen Ashi -- the "X" pattern

Shomen ashi and the two movements that follow it can be seen as an evasion series, due to their similarity to evasion steps in later katas.

To begin Shomen ashi, from the left side, we step forward in tsugiashi (following foot step). As both feet move, the leading foot remains forward and the trailing foot stays behind. Remember to let the center fall into the steps and maintain good posture. In each move of the evasion series, the hands and arms remain relaxed at your sides. The focus here is on the movement of the center and the footwork. Do not rock or tilt, and minimize any bobbing or exaggerated rising or falling action by adjusting with the bend in your knees. Try to remain level in each step.

ICHI   NI   SAN   SHI

GO   ROKU   SHICHI   HACHI

2. Waki Ashi -- side to side

Waki ashi is a side stepping action, and all the same rules apply as in shomen ashi. Pay particular attention not to let the body load up, lean, or tilt in the opposite the direction you are about to step in. In other words, do not prepare to step right by shifting the weight to the left; instead, fall directly into the step from the center. Do not rock or wobble from side to side.

3. Tenkan Ashi -- goblet step

Tenkan ashi is a turning step or "goblet" step. Turn the leading foot in with the hip action closing. Be careful to make no preparatory shifts or foot turnings in the transitions. Turn the leading foot out with a complete opening hip action, and make sure that feet line up square to an imaginary box in front of you and behind you.

4. Shomen Tegatana -- front push

The next five kata forms all employ same hand and foot actions in a variety of ways to deliver energy. The hands and arms are

56

engaged in actions that are recognizable as pushes, parries, pickups, hand changes, and releases. In each form, the arm begins from a relaxed hanging position at your side. As the motion begins, the fingers are engaged first, wrists second, and shoulder last. The hand movement ends at eye level in each action, and the step and arm actions are completed simultaneously. After the forward actions, both left and right, you then turn 90° and repeat them to each side. In this first action, shomen tegatana, just push straight up to eye level with fingers upright and let the hand return to your side as you step back.

5. Uchi Mawashi--inside sweep

In this push from outside to the inside, the footwork and stepping pattern are the same as in the previous form. The arm action begins from the side. As fingers push to the outside, the wrist cocks, and the arm is brought over head in a large outside sweeping action until it descends directly over head to bring the hand, palm pushing out, to eye level. The arm action is like a sword cut coming down on the center line.

6. Soto Mawashi -- underhand push

In this push from the inside to the outside, the footwork and stepping pattern are the same as in the previous two techniques. As the step begins, the fingers engage pointing in, and the wrist pushes forward as the arm moves straight up the center line. The hand sweeps, turning over to a palm up position at eye level at the conclusion of the step.

7. Uchi Soto Gaeshi -- pet the dragon

In this combination of pushes to the inside and then to the outside, the footwork and stepping pattern are the same as in the previous three techniques, but instead of making both front then both side pushes, here we make the front and side push alternately. In the initial step, the hand and arm push to the center line in a horizontal arc ending at eye level. As you step back, the arm returns to the belt line. As the side step begins, the palm rotates up to an outward push, ending at eye level.

8. Uchi Mawashi Gaeshi -- push the sphere

The stepping pattern in this form is across the center line and rotating 180°. This stepping action requires a complete opening and closing of the hips in order to minimize, or even eliminate, any pivoting adjustments of the feet. The pushing hand engages at the side and pushes up in as large an arc as possible. The body rise from the step and the top of the arc of the arm should be simultaneous. As the body drops, the arm falls in a pushing gesture back to the starting point. This series of actions is repeated twice, alternating with each hand.

9. Soto Mawashi Gaeshi -- opposite hand and foot spin

This technique and the two that follow use opposite hand and foot actions that justify themselves by becoming same hand and foot actions. As the step begins, bring the hand up the center line, as in soto mawashi (#6), but using opposite hand and foot. Allow the arm action to extend from overhead into a horizontal sweep to eye level. As the sweep begins, the center rotates 180°; hips should open and close completely in order to minimize steps . The arm action joins the rotation of the center, and the hand terminates palm up at eye level. Finally, raise the hand above head, and raise up on the balls of both feet. This series is repeated on the opposite side.

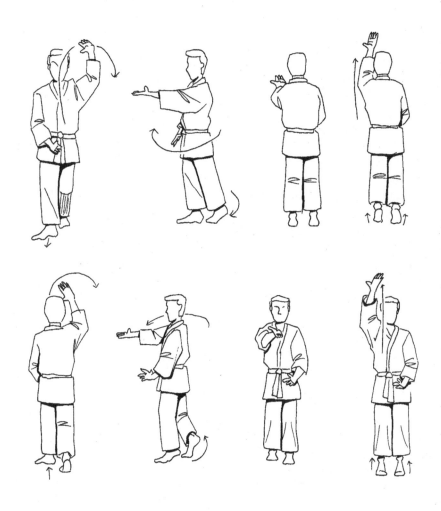

10. Ude Goshi Gaeshi -- hip switch

Ude Goshi Gaeshi is the only technique in the kata in which we use pivoting actions on the balls of our feet. As you step forward, raise the opposite arm, palm up to the center line. Next, engage the fingers and wrist in a downward pushing arc, and begin to pivot 180°. The arm swings down, the hand stays centered, and the body pivots. As the arm swings up into a same hand and foot relationship, the fingers and wrist are in a forward pushing position. Then, reverse all of the above. Make sure that your arm descends and rises in an arc on the vertical plane. There are no horizontal arm actions in this technique. Repeat the series on the opposite side.

11. O Mawashi

O Mawashi is the same move as uchi mawashi gaeshi (#8) but done with opposed hand and foot actions. As you push, step and rotate 180°. The hand and body both rise and fall together. As you return to the starting position, engage both hands in a pushing posture from the center.

12. Yoko O Mawashi -- window wash

With both hands palm out in the center, step to the back corner in a dropping action, and as the body rises, turn back square and return to starting position. The hands will define a horizontal figure eight, which comes from the rise and fall of the body, exaggerated by the bend of the knees not from swinging the arms. Repeat on opposite side.

II. Hanasu no Kata (8 forms of release)

1. Hon Soto Hanasu--normal outside release
2. Hon Soto Te Osu--normal outside hand push
3. Gyaku Soto Hanasu--reverse outside release
4. Gyaku Soto Te Osu--reverse outside hand push
5. Hon Uchi Hanasu--normal inside release
6. Hon Uchi Ude Hineri--normal inside arm twist
7. Gyaku Uchi Hanasu--reverse inside release
8. Gyaku Uchi Hineri--reverse inside arm twist

Hanasu no kata is a fundamental kata for learning evasion and kuzushi (balance breaking), and it is the first exercise in which you get to apply aikido principles in action. The actions of this kata are practiced with uke's making a same hand and foot attack to tori's extended wrist (katate dori). Tori responds at ma-ai and simultaneously evades and takes uke off balance. As uke recovers, tori follows into a fitting position (tsukuri). When practicing the releases, engage the wrist fully into a complete push or curl depending on which technique you are practicing. In the pushing techniques, tori's arm remains unbendable and pivots at the shoulder, like a universal joint; in curling action releases, tori's arm should become like a swinging rope. In either case, power comes from the movement of center, not the action of the arm or upper body.

The kata is structured in a logical progression of repeating patterns. As we study the patterns, we find that #1 and #2 are parallel to #3 and #4 -- the main difference is the side that uke attacks with, either a cross grip (ai gamae) or a mirror side(gyaku gamae) grip. We also find that the second half of the kata are reactions from the first half so that #1 and #5, #2 and #6, #3 and #7, #4 and #8 all form linked pairs of action; whereby, the first release is attempted and altered, or brought about in a modified form. We can see that the 8 releases are an integrated system of actions that build on variations in the basic forms of evasion and off balance.

67

Use of principles in Hanasu no Kata (8 releases)

In each release, tori begins with the arm extended in the lower center (gedan gamae), in same hand and foot relationship, weight even on both feet, in good posture, and with eye contact. Tori evades at ma-ai and maintains aikido principles throughout the movements. All releases are practiced both right and left.

1. Hon Soto Hanasu -- normal outside release

Tori begins with palm down, and as uke attacks with cross grip, tori evades with a pushing gesture to uke's outside. Uke's grip naturally becomes a kote mawashi.

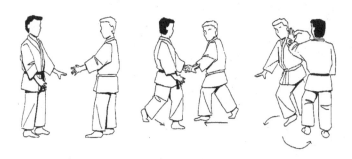

2. Hon Soto Te Osu -- normal outside hand push
Tori begins with palm up, and as uke attacks with cross grip, tori evades with a downward (or turning) pushing gesture to uke's outside. Tori continues to pivot and lets arm swing like rope to uke's full range of motion. Uke's grip and arm position end in an arm coil similar to udegaeshi.

3. Gyaku Soto Hanasu -- reverse outside release

Tori begins with palm up, and as uke attacks with mirror side grip, tori evades in a pushing gesture to uke's outside. Uke's grip naturally becomes a kote mawashi.

4. Gyaku Soto Te Osu -- reverse outside hand push

Tori begins with palm down, and as uke attacks with mirror side grip, tori evades in a curling gesture to uke's outside. Tori continues to pivot and lets arm swing like rope to uke's full range of motion. Tori ends with palm in, and uke's grip and arm position end in udegaeshi.

5. **Hon Uchi Hanasu** -- normal inside release

As in #1, tori begins with palm down, and as uke attacks with cross grip, tori evades with a pushing gesture to uke's outside. Uke tracks to encircle tori. Tori then pivots under uke's attacking arm. Uke's grip and arm position naturally become kote-hineri.

6. **Hon Uchi Ude Hineri** -- normal inside arm twist

As in #2, tori begins with palm up, and as uke attacks with a cross grip, tori evades in a downward pushing gesture to uke's inside. As uke begins to recover, tori pivots under uke's attacking arm causing a spine lock and ending at uke's full range of motion in a shihonage type arm coil.

7. **Gyaku Uchi Hanasu** -- reverse inside release

As in #3, tori begins with palm up, and as uke attacks with mirror side grip, tori evades in a pushing gesture to uke's outside. Uke tracks to encircle tori. Tori then pivots under uke's attacking arm. Uke's grip and arm position naturally become kote-hineri.

8. **Gyaku Uchi Hineri** -- reverse inside arm twist

As in #4, tori begins with palm down, and as uke attacks with a mirror grip, tori evades in a downward pushing gesture to uke's inside. As uke begins to recover, tori pivots under uke's attacking arm causing a spine lock and ending at uke's full range of motion in a shihonage type arm coil.

Notes on the 8 Releases

To understand the concept of the 8 release exercise, we must first consider the unique nature of the attack performed by uke (i.e. grasping at the wrist). The fundamental problem that such an attack offers tori to solve is one of regaining freedom of movement. By grasping tori, uke restricts tori's freedom and potential for response; uke is taking control, and tori must effect some manner of escape or release using off balance and evasion to regain his freedom.

The concept of this form of being attacked should not be treated lightly, for we know from judo that the intent of grasping or gripping our opponent is so that he cannot get away from us as we proceed to off balance and throw him or cause him to submit from being held, arm bared, or choked. It is true that at advanced levels in both judo and aikido, a player may be able to actually execute the throw at the same moment that the grasp is made, in other words, to throw instantaneously with the grip, but in most cases the grasp is made as a preliminary establishment of control.

As tori, we practice escaping from this control in ways that both effect kuzushi in uke and simultaneously move us into a superior strategic position, off the line of the attack. This is why some forms of release action were excluded from this kata; most notably, the inside rising pushes (jodan kuzushi) that we do as the first two techniques of Yon Kata, for while they do effect kuzushi, they do not evade off the line of attack in the initial step and are thus subject to a higher probability of failure.

As we progress in our study of basic release forms, we focus on different applications. Practices vary from teacher to teacher. For instance, in our dojo, for the first few months of training, you will be taught to complete the release action with a push to the face as in shomen ate (This push is a separation technique that we have found useful in giving beginners a realistic form of self- protection). The next application begins at green belt and focuses on leading uke in control positions at the end of the technique. In the brown belt grades, the focus shifts to light following actions, trying to keep the release as light and smooth as possible; when this works, uke feels as if he is grasping air, and tori puts minimum energy into the system. Proceeding on to ikkyu and black belt, the emphasis shifts to the actions of the wrist, the rise and fall of the body, and the effects of these elements on kuzushi (balance breaking). These are just general guidelines of how the different emphasis can be studied, other schools and teachers follow their own regime.

Also, we should note that while these release forms are practiced against the grasp to the wrist, these actions serve equally well against a variety of other attacks. These evasions and balance breaks are completely applicable to many different grasps, strikes, and even kicks. In addition, once the basic forms have been internalized, the forms themselves can be varied significantly by tori -- such forms include active forms in which tori grasps uke and effects wrist locks, and also forms that either shorten or lengthen uke's steps. All such application can be explored at advanced level, but for daily training, the focus should remain on the basic kata forms, for it is in this form that we train to establish the maximum degree of safety against the most technically difficult attacks.

As we progress through the releases, we learn to practice them from certain hand positions. We know that at advanced levels you can naturally flow into virtually any release from any hand position and that all releases can be started from a "neutral" or handshake position; however, in our early training, we find it helpful to develop these releases from the extreme palm up and palm down positions so that we may condition our hand action reflexes to respond to the worst positions possible, i.e. at the naturally effective limits of our wrist's range of motion. By training in this way, we are protecting ourselves in case we are grabbed while our hands are in one of these vulnerable positions. By training in the worst position, we learn the ways we can still function, but if we were to always work from a superior or neutral position, and were then faced with a worst case situation, we might be in trouble, since we had depended on a crutch of superior position in our training.

As we are grasped in the extreme palm up or palm down position, it becomes clear that we are also teaching our nervous system to react differently to stimuli on the outside of the wrist and stimuli on the inside. Additionally, we learn to feel the difference, and react to it, when grasped from the cross hand or mirror hand positions and which wrist actions and directions allow us to function efficiently and which are dead ends. Upon reflection, we find that this kata has provided us with curling and pushing actions that are most appropriate for any permutation of grasping attacks, all of which become unconsciously triggered by the stimulus of different grips to different areas of the wrist.

If we are to really excel in the practice of release forms, we must concentrate, as tori, on matching the rhythm of uke's body rise and fall in each step. We must also match uke's speed, both of the body, the feet, and of the gripping hand, as closely as possible. If we are successful, this blending of rhythm and speed results in depriving uke of any sensory feedback that he could react to or against, and we will achieve "tactile invisibility." This invisibility of touch occurs because the relative speed between tori and uke becomes zero. Uke only feels a "sameness" -- no push or pull, only a sense of grasping at air, paradoxically coupled with the sensation of having a grip on your wrist. Uke can feel the wrist, the skin and bones, but not the motion, and without a sense of motion or direction, uke quickly looses control.

Hanasu no Kata is also the first kata in which the application of eye contact becomes a critical factor, for with this principle we have an automatic means of alignment of our centered action to uke's center line, so no matter where or how uke moves we remain fixed on his center and capable of delivering energy to this line at any moment. Thus, eye contact virtually eliminates the need to aim.

Particular attention should be paid to posture, especially in the last four releases in which there is a tendency to lean or duck under uke's arm. We must not loose proper posture while effecting the technique. Make up for height differences by bending the knees, not the back.

Lastly, we should keep in mind that this kata is in the form of exercises to control balance and fit with reactions. The eight release kata is not meant to be a kata of throws -- though with an uke who attacks with too much strength or speed or who has not yet learned how to efficiently recover balance, falls are almost inevitable.

Note on technical variations

When we teach, it is wise to often stress that there are no absolute right or wrong ways to apply any given technique. Of course, there are forms that are closer to a standard kata form, meaning closer to the middle of the technical window, but in any given technique, there are a range of options that are all viable to varying degrees. The kata form of the techniques we practice is approximately in the center of this range or window of viability. In this way, if you deviate somewhat from this middle form (and under stress we all deviate), then you still are left with a reasonable chance of having a viable technique, but if you had always trained in some extreme form, on the edge of the window and had deviated, then your chances of failure would be much greater. Its easy to see that if we are trying to build a realistic and automatic self -defense, then we should internalize these "central" forms and spend most of our time repeating these forms, but this preference for practice does not make them any more "right" than any of the other more extreme ideas. In fact, in any given technique, we find an extraordinary range of technical variations that are all completely viable (they just are not necessarily the forms you should internalize), and exploring these variations is part of what makes the study of aikido so fascinating. As you continue your aikido training, you will no doubt run across many of these technical variations, and it is only human nature to set up some as better or worse, right or wrong, but we should always try to remember that far from being a limited black and white issue, it is the great variety of interpretation that makes for the true art form, and it is the mature artist who can appreciate the subtle artistic qualities and variations as he explores his field.

III. Ju Nana Hon Kata

17 Main Forms -- or Randori no Kata
Atemi Waza (striking techniques)
1. Shomen-Ate -- forward strike
2. Aigamae-Ate --regular posture   strike
3. Gyakugamae-Ate -- reverse posture strike
4. Gedan-Ate -- low strike
5. Ushiro-Ate --behind strike

Hiji Waza (elbow techniques)
6. Oshi-Taoshi -- push down
7. Ude-Gaeshi -- arm reversal
8. Hiki-Taoshi -- pull and push down
9. Ude-Hineri -- arm twist
10. Waki-Gatame -- side arm lock

Tekubi Waza (wrist techniques)
11. Kote-Hineri -- wrist twist
12. Kote-Gaeshi -- wrist reversal
13. Tenkai-Kote-Hineri --pivoting wrist turn
14. Shiho-Nage -- four corner throw

Uki Waza (floating techniques)
15. Mae-Otoshi -- forward drop
16. Sumi-Otoshi -- rear corner drop
17. Hiki-Otoshi -- pull and drop

Ju Nana Hon Kata -- Introduction and Discussion

The next kata to consider is Ju Nana Hon Kata or the seventeen kata of basic throws and control techniques. This kata is also referred to as randori no kata by some schools; for simplicity, this text will refer to it as the Seventeen.

This kata is the technical heart of the requirements for first degree black belt, and in truth, this kata allows us to build and

77

internalize fundamental throwing and controlling principles that are then utilized both in randori, in which we find the realistic application of these movements, and in the higher kata, in which we see repeated variations on these themes. Interestingly, the seventeen waza or techniques of this kata are actually a distillation from the higher old style (koryu) forms that were refined for usage in realistic randori application.

The kata is divided into technical sections that begin with controlling and attacking the center line of uke's body and progressively moving out to the shoulder, the elbow, and the wrist from there. Shihan Karl Geis has said that an essential component of this kata is that all techniques are characterized by tori's center moving towards uke's center as the technique is applied.

The first section of the kata is the Atemi waza or striking techniques. As Professor Kenji Tomiki pointed out, the focus of atemi waza in the past, generally, has been forms of hitting, thrusting, or kicking to the physiologically weak points of the anatomy. There is, however, a second form of atemi waza; whereby, the opponent is thrown by pushing or grasping the mechanically weak points of the body (as in balance breaking or kuzushi). The striking techniques in the seventeen all utilize this second principle of atemi. They take the form of pushes and pulls applied to uke's head, shoulders, and torso all done in a non-percussive manner, and in fact, these strikes can be executed in a passive form, as separation techniques, rather than active throws. We have found that often, when these forms are used in real self-defense situations, they unfold as such separation actions, actions that keep safety and distance, and any fall that occurs is a consequence of the attacker's own momentum and reflex action, rather than the defender's intent to throw. In other words, the attacker will often throw himself, in effect; while all the defender is doing is attempting to keep separation and safety. Of course, we train to commit these throws in an active and decisive way, but this commitment is simply a form of fail safe or back up to the primary defensive separation concept, so that if separation fails, and you are forced to throw the person to save your skin, you will be quite capable.

The next sections deal with controlling techniques that utilize joint locks. Again, Professor Tomiki has discussed that in the past, these kansetsu waza or joint lock techniques were used to control an opponent by causing sprain and dislocation on a joint; the aim being to maim or injure the attacker. But, in a more refined form, these techniques can be used to restrain an opponent with a minimum of force by utilizing the limits of a joint's range of motion. In fact, in the forms we practice, we do not apply these forms as pain techniques, nor do we allow "cranking" or any use of brute force against the joints. The locks are taken gently to the uke's limit of motion and then restrained. Again, any injury that occurs results from the attacker's attempt to resist the restraint, not from the defender's intent to do damage.

The first section of kansetsu waza deal with locks and throws involving the shoulder and elbow and is called Hiji waza or arm lock techniques. The second section deals with locks and throws that involve the wrist joint and are called Tekubi waza. The final section, Uki waza, or floating techniques, are techniques that combine joint locks with techniques of floating or moving with uke's momentum and resistance to effect throws.

As we examine the seventeen in more detail, we find that throughout the kata there are several obvious "linked" techniques, techniques that flow from one to the other and are based on uke's reactions. In the atemi waza section, we find Gyakugame-ate (#3) and Gedan-ate (#4). In the Hiji waza section, we have Oshi-taoshi (#6) and its reaction Udegaeshi(#7) followed by Hikitaoshi(#8) and its reaction Udehineri (#9). The linked forms continue, for in the Tekubi waza section we have Kotehineri (#11) and its reaction Kotegaeshi(#12). Finally in the Uki waza we find each technique linked in series, all beginning with the Shihonage(#14) balance break, and progressing logically from Maeotoshi(#15), to Sumiotoshi (#16), to Hikiotoshi(#17).

In addition to these linked forms, there are also some more subtle pairings that can be made. These pairings are not so much reaction links, but more correlations or parallels in form. For instance, we can see a positional correlation between the initial off balance in

79

Shomenate and the off balance in the Shihonage series; between Aigameate, with its control of the elbow, and Oshitaoshi; we can see Gyakugameate in a reversed form as Hikitaoshi; the beginning of Ushiroate as an potential entrance for Tenkai-Kotehineri. The more we look, the more parallels we find. Such linkages, correlations, and parallels are indicative of the riai (The synergy of logical principles) of the kata, and we can see how the kata is a work of remarkable genius, as the form builds on its own concepts with variations both in the initial conditions of tori's actions and in uke's reactions. Shihan Karl Geis has pointed out that this kata is "uke driven" and that tori implements techniques only as uke's reaction dictates. This sensitivity to uke is coupled with an awareness of the initial conditions of tori -- particularly whether or not tori grips uke, and if so, what form and on what part of the wrist or hand the grasp is made. Such conditions all become driving factors for determining what technique follows. In any case, we see that small changes in the initial conditions of tori's actions and uke's reactions are the determining factors of these techniques.

Finally, as in the 8 releases, tori should strive to match uke's speed and rhythm as closely as possible and try to apply the basic principles consistently throughout the various techniques.

Historical Note on Ju Nana Hon Kata

Ju Nana Hon Kata is also known as Randori no Kata and grew out of Professor Tomiki's research into rikakutaisei waza (techniques used when at a distance from the opponent). In 1936, Jigoro Kano, the founder of Judo, approached Mr. Tomiki about the possibility of including the aiki-budo techniques that Tomiki had been studying as a part of the judo curriculum. Kano had observed a demonstration by Ueshiba in 1930 and is reported to have said, "This is my ideal judo!" Kano hoped to include the aiki techniques as "rikakutaisei " or hamare judo (judo at a distance), but was concerned that the task of making the practice into a safe and logical form would prove impossible. Just before Professor Tomiki left for a teaching post in

80

Manchuria, he assured Kano that by applying Kano's own analytic principles, he felt sure that a system could be devised that would allow the safe practice of aiki in the judo randori form. The Kodokan Judo Institute began a research program into rikakutaisei with Tomiki's research leading the forefront. Tomiki published the results of his research in 1944, but events of the war interfered with his progress. After the war, Tomiki continued to pursue Kano's rikakutaisei idea, and from it he developed goshin jutsu no kata (kata of self defense) which integrates aikido and judo techniques and which was adopted as a formal kata of Kodokan Judo. Eventually in the early 1950's, Professor Tomiki began teaching " a practical course in judo exercises" at Waseda University. These exercises included 12 prototypical forms of aikido randori techniques, which later became 15, and eventually the 17 we know today. These forms were the product of Tomiki's long years of research and study and were in fact a distillation of Ueshiba's original forms of aikido waza that had undergone the rigors of the analysis that had previously been common only in judo. Indeed, in the late fifties, Ueshiba requested that Tomiki bring his system back to the Hombu dojo (Ueshiba's headquarters), but Ueshiba's inner circle eventually rejected Tomiki's research and refused to adopt his approach to aikido training. Consequently, in 1960 Tomiki ryu aikido began.

Ju Nana Hon Kata-- described on right side only

1. Shomen ate

Tori evades leading with right foot in an inside goblet step while bringing up right hand palm forward to the inside of uke's wrist.

Uke attacks from ma-ai with unbendable arm in same hand and foot with tsugiashi from the right directly to tori's chin.

Tori brings left hand underneath right hand and executes hand change as left foot adjusts in a following action behind right foot.

Uke recovers from evasion and begins to track or square up to tori so as to prepare for a secondary attack.

The free right hand moves directly to uke's chin as right step commences forward.
Tori completes right step in tsugiashi -- stepping usually between uke's feet for the throw.

With chin up, uke's spine is locked by hand on chin.
Uke prepares for back fall.
Back fall.

Pause and watch uke as uke returns to standing for the next technique.

Stand up and reset distance and position for next attack.

Notes on Shomen ate

This waza is deceptive in its simplicity, for contained in this simple little throw are issues of subtle kuzushi, hand and body placement, control of ma-ai and a termination in perhaps the most powerful throw possible. Shomen ate is such a strong throw that it acts as our fail safe for self defense, and at its terminal point (kake), it has been found to have the greatest probability of success of all aikido throws. Elegant in its simplicity, yet complex in its issues, this waza requires us to "walk on the edge of the world" as Shihan Geis puts it. In this, Shomen ate well fits the description of what Donn Draeger describes as "physical koan, or conundrum … a situation that evokes technical crisis," for we begin our action of entrance by making a nearly fatal error (entering to the inside of the arm), and from here we must first survive and next prevail from this very inferior position. By learning to work from the worst possible position, and excel, we find it easier to function in all the more superior positions. That is why this simple little beginner's technique, is probably the most technically advanced.

2. **Aigamae ate**

Tori evades to the right front corner while using both hands in unbendable arm position, stepping with right foot leading tsugiashi, to effect a balance break -- hands contact uke's outer wrist and do not grasp.

Uke attacks from ma-ai with right hand as in previous technique.

Uke's balance and posture are broken to the left side.

Tori slides left hand to control uke's elbow and brings right hand to uke's chin from underneath the arm ; simultaneously, the left foot follows behind the right as the left hand moves so that tori can effect a right side tsugiashi and push to throw.

Uke begins to recover balance.

Uke's chin is up and spine is locked back; uke prepares for Back fall. Back fall.

Pause and keep focused on uke as uke returns to standing position.

Stand up, re-set ma-ai, and position for next technique.

Notes on Aigame ate

The two critical elements here are the balance break -- done stepping
forward down the line of the feet, using unbendable arms, both hands
in center – and the hand change to control uke's elbow. The hands
begin at uke's wrist and as the uke turns in recovery of balance, tori
allows the inside or mirror side hand to slide up the forearm and take
control just above uke's elbow. From this control position, tori can
safely execute the throw

3. Gyakugamae ate

Uke attacks as in #2

Tori evades and breaks balance as in #2 but lightly grasps uke's wrist with the little finger of the right hand in a yoke, that slightly extends the kuzushi and forces a larger recovery.

Uke's balance is broken to the left front corner and extended. Recovery takes the form of body rise.

With free left hand, tori pushes laterally through uke's forehead, catching uke at the peak of body rise and using left side step in tsugiashi to throw.

As uke recovers up, the spine is locked back by either the eye threat or by tori's contact at forehead.

Uke prepares for Back fall. Back fall.

* Note*
On occasion, this throw is executed as an eye threat rather than a simple push. The difference is primarily dependent on uke's reactions.

Notes on Gyakugame ate

In this technique we again begin with the standard balance break and as uke rises in recovery we follow his body rise with a push/eye threat. The eye threat concept works off of the body's natural reflex to pull the head violently back when and object rapidly closes in on its eyes. To accentuate the rise and provoke the reaction it is helpful (but not always necessary) to yoke uke's wrist with the leading hand in the balance break. As uke's attempts to recover from the initial kuzushi, he will be pulling against the yoke and setting up the line of tension down which the eye threat will have maximum effect.

4. Gedan ate

Tori begins as in #3 with gyakugame ate.

Tori controls the rising arm upward with a yoked grasp and slides left hand across uke's center in a push in order to prevent a secondary attack from uke's left side -- tori's hand should be at or near uke's left inner elbow, and tori's left foot floats in tsugiashi **behind** uke's right leg, so as to fit in snugly and lock uke's spine back.

Tori steps through uke in a side step with left tsugiashi to throw.

Note
Tori's posture is critical as the fit in is made. Tori must not duck under uke's arm or bend forward. Tori's action should be expansive, stretching uke out from his wrist to his hips. Do not twist or turn backward to throw uke over the left leg.

Uke attacks as in #3.

As tori attempts balance break for gyakugame ate, uke resists by bringing the right arm up to block the eye threat.
Uke's balance is broken in a spine lock backward.

Uke steps with left foot into a side fall.

Note on Gedan ate

This waza is response to a failed gyakugame ate. As tori attempts the
eye threat, uke forces a technical crisis by blocking the hand. The
rising block also makes tori vulnerable to an attack from uke's
second hand (particularly if it held a weapon). Tori must resolve this
problem decisively by taking uke into the spine locked control
position while controlling the threat of the secondary attack. Once
the gap is closed and uke's spine is locked, tori can then execute the
throw by stepping through uke. Avoid any twisting idea in the throw
since this twisting form has a high degree of failure when executed
on a larger, stronger opponent.

5. Ushiro ate

Tori evades left (left foot leading) with goblet step and uses right hand in a light sliding parry up uke's arm toward the center.

Uke attacks as in all previous techniques.
Uke's balance is slightly disturbed to the front/left by the evasion and parry.

Tori continues to slide up uke's arm using a tenkan action going behind uke until both hands come to uke's shoulders where they hook downward with the palms as if reaching for the collarbones.

Uke continues to recover forward and to the left.

Spine is locked back by hands hooking at the shoulders.

Uke prepares for Back fall.

Tori continues to rotate with tenkan action into the throw.

Back fall.

Note on Ushiro ate

We begin this technique by stepping on the wrong foot (as our right hand makes contact at the wrist, our left foot is stepping around), we have broken the same hand and foot principle, and this waza provides us with a useful means to survive this very common predicament. Make sure that tori's hand slides all the way up uke's arm to the shoulder without breaking contact. After Shomen ate, this technique may be the most common in randori.

6. Oshi Taoshi

Tori effects right front corner balance break with both hands lightly grasping the outside of uke's wrist.

Uke attacks in standard form. Balance and posture are broken to the left front corner.
Uke begins to recover and resists by pulling against grip.

As uke pulls, tori floats back and cycles feet to establish left hand and foot forward with left hand sliding up the forearm for control on uke's elbow.
Elbow is locked up in a line pushing through uke's ear.

As right elbow is locked up, uke's body rises and off balance occurs to the left corner into a forward fall.

Uke is locked face down with elbow and shoulder restrained.

Tori follows uke's front fall, maintaining light control of the elbow until it straightens naturally as uke becomes prone. Uke's arm is brought beyond 90° of the shoulder joint and gentle pressure is applied to elbow with body drop.

Submit by patting out (mairi).

Note on Oshi taoshi

The technical problem that uke provokes by his arm pulling reaction is a crisis in tori's footwork. Tori must learn to float back with the lead foot so as to establish same hand and foot relationship. Simultaneously, tori must allow the inside hand to slide up uke's forearm and find the elbow. To execute the throw without injuring uke requires that we push through uke's centerline
(i.e. push the elbow through the ear). Lock the arm at shoulder level or above. Never use excessive force in establishing or holding arm bars.

7. Ude Gaeshi

Same as in oshi taoshi (#6)

Standard attack.

As tori attempts to off balance and control the elbow, uke resists with a downward pull and recovery step.

Tori follows uke's resistance back to full balance break position, maintaining light control on elbow.

As pull continues, uke's arm curls.

As uke curls arm, tori guides uke's wrist in a coil around tori's left hand -- "threading the needle"

As arm coils and is stretched up and out, off balance takes place to the rear.

Uke's coiled arm is extended with left hand in a pushing gesture high and to uke's back corner as the right hand maintains wrist yoke.

Uke prepares for Back fall.

Back fall.

Tori extends coil into a Back fall and follows uke to the ground in a knelling position, locking coiled arm bar with left hand and prepares for shomen strike from overhead.

Uke submits from arm lock by patting out (mairi).

Note on Ude gaeshi

This technique follows on a failed attempt to execute the throw in oshi taoshi and causes tori to float back into balance break position while following the natural function of uke's resistance into the arm coil. As uke pushes free of oshi taoshi, tori follows and maintains a light touch at the elbow with the inside hand while yoking with the lead hand. As uke rises, tori's turning action produces the backward coil with the elbow hand becoming the axis around which the coil occurs. Uke is spine locked and controlled primarily by the pushing hand in the arm coil, not the yoking hand at the wrist lock. Throw is executed primarily by pushing back, not curling down.

8. Hiki Taoshi

Standard attack.

Tori executes an evasive balance break to the right front corner with both hands yoking uke's wrist in an outside butterfly position.

Off balance occurs to uke's left front.

Tori swings into alignment with uke's arm controlling with the left hand yoke and releases right hand to an upward moving eye threat.

Uke begins to rise in recovery of posture.
Eye threat causes rise to be exaggerated as head moves back.

Off balance occurs to the right front corner as tori tractors back.

Tori steps back with left foot leading in a reversed tsugiashi while tractoring uke's arm.

Uke falls forward.

As uke descends forward, tori lightly controls elbow with right hand.
As uke comes to the prone position on the floor, the arm is restrained beyond 90° of the shoulder joint.

Uke submits to arm bar.

Note
Tori must maintain dynamic tension on the pulling arm, using his own arm like a rope and not allowing any slack as he backs away.

Note on Hiki taoshi

There are only two fundamental ways of delivering energy with the human body, pushing and pulling. Up until now these kata techniques have been primarily making use of pushing, but in this waza we execute by pulling (not with the arm but with the whole body). After our initial balance break using the out side butterfly grip, we step around the front corner of uke and are in clear danger of being overwhelmed; we are forced to keep separation with the eye threat and step back. As we do so the yoked arm pulls taught like a rope, and uke topples forward.

9. Ude Hineri

Same as in Hiki taoshi (#8)

Tori responds to uke's pull by floating into a push with the left hand and foot advancing, which drives the arm behind uke's back.

Standard attack.
Same as in hiki taoshi. As tori swings in line with arm and begins eye threat, uke resists off balance by pulling back with the arm.

Tori's right hand slides over uke's dropping shoulder and reinforces the locking action.
Tori is now beside uke, parallel but facing the opposite direction.

As arm is driven back into the lock, uke's body coils forward in off balance and left foot moves forward.

Lock is secured to uke's hip for safety.

Tori performs hip switch, pushing through the locked arm and hip to throw.

As tori hip switches, uke is pushed into forward off balance and rolling break fall.

98

Note on Ude hineri

As tori attempts to throw hiki taoshi, uke succeeds in overwhelming tori by pulling back himself. Tori is forced to reverse himself and float into uke's side. As tori is pulled, he must allow his outside leg to lead and step as close to parallel to uke's line as possible. Older forms locked the arm in a reverse mawashi, but this was abandoned due to the high risk of injury to the shoulder. Uke's wrist is now secured to his hip and the power of the hip switch is delivered on the side of the hip itself.

10. Waki Gatame

Uke makes standard attack.

Tori makes right step evasive balance break while gripping wrist in an upward butterfly with both hands. Tori's thumbs in uke's palm.

Uke's posture and balance broken to the front left.

Tori continues to advance in right side tsugiashi 45°, down the line of uke's feet.

Uke is continuing in off-balance toward the back left side, body has turned. Posture was degenerated.

As tori advances and pushes, the angle between tori's and uke's arms close naturally until tori's elbow rests gently against uke's elbow.

Controlling with the left hand at the wrist, tori establishes the lock using the crook of the right elbow to extend into the full lock. Left arm applies downward pressure on uke's triceps. Gentle pressure is applied by expanding the chest and solar plexus against the elbow and by lowering the center by allowing the right foot to gradually widen the stance.

As lock is established, uke's posture bends forward slightly.

Submission from standing by patting out (mairi).

100

Note on Waki gatame

As tori pushes through in the balance break, uke's elbow natural rotates over and becomes exposed. Tori continues to close the gap and draws uke out on the line square to his feet. This secondary balance break on the perpendicular line is often neglected, but allows for much greater control of uke with a minimum of force. As the inside hand controls the wrist into the yoke of the outside elbow, maintain pressure on uke's triceps, just above his elbow. Do not let this arm bar devolve into an upper body strength contest. The lock is the by-product of the body positions not the tension of the arms and shoulder muscles.

11. Kote Hineri

Balance break is the same as oshitaoshi (#6) except that the grip is established with the right hand on the outer edge of uke's hand.

Uke makes standard attack.

Same as in oshi taoshi.

As uke resists by pulling, tori follows into foot cycle and establishes elbow block and inward turned wrist lock.

Body rise is exaggerated by elbow and wrist lock.

Throw is with the left hand leading, pushing through the ear as in oshi taoshi while maintaining a floating control of the wrist lock.

Same as in oshi taoshi -- front fall into face down position.

Wrist lock is gently applied once uke is prone and the arm has reached the limit of the range of motion in this coil.

Submission by patting out (mairi).

Note on Kote hineri

In this technique we are facing virtually the same issues as in oshi taoshi, but here we are asked to be even more fine tuned in our response to uke's reaction of pulling. As uke pulls up in recovery, tori floats into the foot cycle to establish same hand and foot and simultaneously lets the inside hand slide up the fore arm to the elbow, and also follows into a turned in wrist control with the secondary hand. We are not twisting the wrist, but following it in a push to the end of its natural range of motion. The throw is executed as in oshi taoshi with wrist control maintained all of the way through.

12. Kote Gaeshi

Same as in kote hineri (#11)

Standard attack.

Tori follows uke's resistance back to full balance break position while maintaining grip on outside of uke's hand with right hand.

As tori attempts to establish elbow and wrist lock, uke resists by pushing out with a recovery step.

As uke completes recovery step, tori pivots around uke's hand and feeds his right grip into his left hand to establish an outward turned wrist coil. Right hand then reinforces the coil as tori extends uke down the line of the extended arm and over the coiled wrist.

Uke completes recovery step and begins to body rise into the next step.

As wrist is coiled, off balance occurs to the right front corner. As tori extends down the line of the arm, uke performs an elevated rolling break fall.

Tori maintains control as uke falls and locks an outward turning wrist and arm coil against the outer thigh.

Submission (mairi).

Note on Kote gaeshi

This is perhaps the most popular and most abused aikido throw. Countless styles throw this by cranking the wrist, twisting the wrist, or by compressing the extensor tendons by pressing the fingers down. All of these variations are painful, injurious, and inefficient The true power of kote gaeshi to flip uke in the air comes from the extension of uke's step off balance while his body is being held in a asymmetrical coil, not from twisting the wrist hard.

13. Tenkai Kote Hineri

Tori makes left side evasion as a goblet step. Grip with outside butterfly yoke at the wrist.

Uke makes standard attack. Uke tracks and begins to turn toward tori in body rise.

As uke turns, tori executes hand change, right hand feeding left with hip switch.

As hip switch occurs, uke's balance and posture are broken forward. Uke begins to recover in body rise.

As uke rises, tori follows in a tenkan action and raises uke's wrist in a high yoke with the left hand. At the peak of body rise, wrist lock is established with the left hand gripping while the right hand comes free as turn continues, and as the arm is brought down to hip level, the right hand closes gently on the elbow. As arm is descending, tori makes a pivoting foot action in order to step square in front of uke, eye to eye. The wrist, elbow and shoulder lock down in a sweeping action to establish the final lock with uke prone.

Uke is extended up at peak of body rise and coiled downward and backward as body descends.

Uke submits in face down position with wrist lock and arm coil (mairi).

Note on Tenkai kote hineri

This is another heavily abused technique in the aikido world. And again the problem comes from turning it into a pain-compliance technique, rather than an off balance technique. Most styles execute this wrist lock by twisting and stressing the flexor tendons in the wrist and fingers. They crank in and up in a way that causes pain and injury. The true power of this technique comes from the rotation of the body coupled with the asymmetrical leverage on the shoulder joint. The wrist is merely held in a position to maximize the leverage as the body turns and arm drops. This is such a powerful method that in most cases the wrist lock is completely secondary and the technique could be made just as easily while grasping the forearm. Incidentally, practitioners of the pain theory of joint locks also stand a very high chance of being countered and overpowered by anyone with a bit of strength and a high pain threshold.

14. Shiho Nage (Tenkai Kotegaeshi)

Uke makes standard attack.

Tori evades to the right with inside goblet step, yoking uke's wrist with inside butterfly grip.

Uke begins to recover from evasion and track tori.

Tori executes hand change with hip switch, left hand feeding right, to coil uke's arm.

Uke's balance is broken in a body turn to the back left corner as the arm is coiled.

Tori extends the coiled arm, pushing forward with left step forward, then makes hip switch reversal while always maintaining high extended push on arm coil.

As uke rises in recovery, off balance occurs from the hip switch to the back corner causing spine lock.

Uke prepares for back fall.

Tori extends arm coil with push from right hand and foot and follows uke down into back fall, settling into coiled wrist lock from knelling and threatening with high shomen strike position with left hand.

Back fall.

Submission from wrist coil (mairi).

Note on Shiho nage

In this waza we confront a very similar crisis to that posed by
shomen ate, for again we have stepped to the inside (a dangerous
place to be), but this time, to make matters worse, our hands are in an
awkward position and we are unable to make separation by pushing
the face. Tori must save himself with a hip switch and continue the
rotation around with a second hip switch. The throw is executed not
by twisting or cranking down on the wrist, but by pushing out
through the arm coil.

15. Mae Otoshi

Tori makes same evasion and balance break as in shihonage (#14).

Standard attack.
Uke is coiled off balance as in shiho nage, but uke attempts to evade to the rear as the arm coil is established.

Tori floats with the coil, locking wrist with right hand and coiling elbow with left hand.

Uke is forced into exaggerated body rise by arm coil.

As uke begins to move off of body rise, tori uncoils uke's arm and pushes through the diagonal line of uke's step with a sliding, dropping push from the left hand, driving uke into a forward roll as the right hand is released.

Uke is unbalanced forward to the left and performs rolling break fall.

Note on Mae otoshi

This technique follows along after tori attempts shiho nage and at the end of the first hip switch, uke turns away and attempts to pull free. The arm coil is held and uke's turning causes him to exaggerate his body rise. Tori follows the rise and then executes the throw as uke's arm uncoils and his body drops. We are not cranking the wrist, uke's own reactions take him into the coil.

16. Sumi Otoshi

Same as in mae otoshi (#15)

Standard attack.

Same as mae otoshi, but as tori coils arm, uke resists by pulling the arm back in a step with the right foot.

Tori floats with uke's pull until momentum ceases then extends with tsugiashi step in an inverted wrist coil to throw to the corner that uke has pulled to.

Balance is broken to the right front corner.
Elevated rolling break fall.

Note on Sumi otoshi

Here uki is reacting to the arm coil from mae otoshi by reversing with a pull so as to get behind tori's arm and possibly reverse the throw. As tori follows uke's pull and turn, make sure to maintain good separation between the bodies. The throw is executed with an extension of uke's step which requires tori to follow slightly behind and throw by exploiting the metatarsal reflex as in kotegaeshi.

17. **Hiki Otoshi**

Standard attack.

Same as in sumi otoshi (#16)

As arm is coiled, uke pulls and tracks in to square up with tori so as to attack from the left.

Tori floats back to the inside of uke's arm and executes hand change so that left hand slides down to control uke's wrist while the right hand slides up to control the elbow in a vertical arm bar.

As arm bar is established, uke's forward momentum is halted in a body rise.

Tori extends uke's arm down the line of uke's feet in a dropping action of the left knee. As tori drops and extends, the right hand slides down to reinforce the drop. Uke is thrown in an elevated rolling break fall.

As tori extends and drops, uke's balance is broken forward in an elevated break fall.

Note on Hiki otoshi

In this case, uke is turning back in to counter tori head on -- he is overwhelming tori, pressing him, and tori must respond by changing control hands, stepping back for separation, and locking the elbow; all just to keep uke off of him. The crisis continues, for uke's momentum is still coming forward and tori is in its path. Tori drops down and away from the oncoming momentum, thereby triggering the metatarsal reflex and fall.

IV. Owaza Ju Pon (the Big Ten)

1. **Kata Otoshi**
2. **Kubi Garuma**
3. **Ude Garuma**
4. **Hiji Garuma**
5. **Aiki Nage**
6. **Shiho Nage**
7. **Ushiro Ate**
8. **Kote gaeshi**
9. **Ushiro Kubi Gatame**
10. **Shizumi Otoshi**

The Big Ten, or 10 Defensive Throws, are the advanced throws that we learn as we approach first degree black belt. Shihan Geis has described the defining principle of this kata as being that the throws are executed as tori's center is moving away from uke's center. He has also stressed that this kata's initial condition in foot work is different than in the 17. Both katas function as if tori were walking normally at the moment of attack. But in Ju Nana Hon Kata, the footwork is predicated on the assumption that the balance break is taking place **as your lead foot is descending from the peak of body rise and heading to the floor**. Consequently, in the 17, all tori can do is extend the step or shorten the step into tsugi ashi and balance break. However, in the Big Ten, we find tori just as **he is about to begin to pick up his back foot and go toward the peak of body rise.** Since tori must react as he is rising with the movement of the back foot, we see in this kata a number of turning evasions and balance breaks.

The Owaza Ju Pon is an amazingly dynamic kata and shows its differences clearly in the number of garuma (wheel action) throws that occur in the first half. This new form of ukemi is demanding on uke and also forces tori to learn a new application for throwing into elevated break falls.

116

First of all, in the garuma fall, the uke is turned not only in one direction, toward the floor as in kote gaeshi or sumiotoshi, but also uke is rotated like a wheel horizontally spinning. This convergence of forces can be very disorienting and challenging for uke at first; consequently, you would be wise to use safety mats when learning the ukemi for these throws.

Secondly, the form of these throws are expansive and thus require tori to continue to stay in motion longer than is customary in similar throws in the Seventeen. For instance, as tori throws uke in sumi otoshi from the 17, tori will become static as uke becomes airborne, but in the similar technique of hiji garuma from the Big 10, tori must continue to pull and float back in a circular manner until uke has landed. In fact, the continuation of the added vector of force while uke is airborne gives these throws their distinctive character.

Also, it should be noted that many teachers describe this kata as a form of reacting to uke once uke has penetrated ma-ai. For what ever reason, tori has reacted late and now must try to get away from this dangerous situation. In essence, the throws occur as last ditch attempts to survive a bad situation.

Owaza Ju Pon -- Technical descriptions
Techniques are described only from the right side. Always learn and
practice both sides.

Tori begins in a mirror side stance to uke.

1. Kata Otoshi
As uke attacks from ma-ai, tori goblet steps with right foot leading
inside uke's line. Tori's left hand makes an open hand touch to uke's
forearm while the right hand blocks the front/top of uke's near
shoulder, tori continues to rotate from the goblet step. The shoulder
check on uke prevents the completion of uke's foot cycle, and as
tori's turn is completed, uke is pitched forward by the pendulum
action of tori's rear leg (tori's left leg swinging back has the identical
effect as if the right leg had swung forward).

2. Kubi Garuma

Uke attacks and tori responds the same as in #1, but as tori steps in, he establishes a grip on uke's inside wrist with the left hand and uses the right as a cupping hook to the back of uke's neck. As tori rotates his center through the line that uke is on, uke is taken into the garuma by tori's moving away from uke's position in rotation. Tension in the arms stays constant. Tori continues to move and rotate until uke has landed.

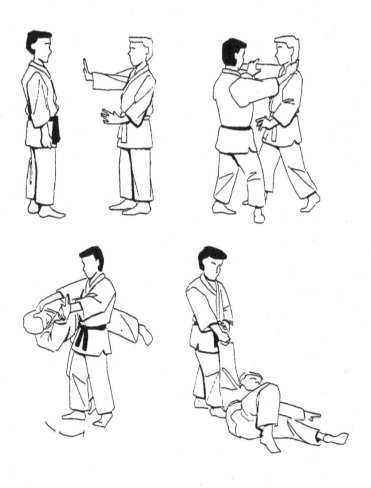

3. Ude Garuma

Same as in #2, but as tori steps in, he establishes a grip on uke's inside wrist with the left hand and uses the right hand to grip the upper arm. The rotation and form of the throw as a garuma are the same as in #2, only the rotation is slightly more open due to the difference in grip position.

4. Hiji Garuma

Same as in #3, but as tori steps in, he establishes a grip on uke's inside wrist with the left hand, and uses the right hand to grip the forearm just below the elbow. Form and effect of garuma are the same as #3, but the rotation is even more open because of the change in hand position.

Tori now assumes a cross stance to uke.

5. **Aiki Nage** (Aiki Garuma)

As uke attacks from ma-ai, tori evades, right foot leading to uke's outside, similar to ushiro ate. Tori rotates into uke from behind with the left arm draped over uke's left shoulder and right arm covering uke's right arm. Tori's backward rotation draws uke down and around in a spiral. As uke recovers and rises up, tori reverses direction of rotation to bring right hand over uke's left shoulder from the front to lock uke's spine back and twisting to the inside. Tori continues to rotate through uke, and uke falls out from under the arm in an unassisted garuma fall. Tori continues to rotate until uke has landed.

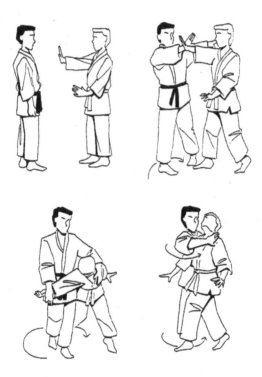

6. Shiho Nage

As uke attacks from ma-ai, tori breaks balance with a back step and inside butterfly to uke's left front corner. On uke's recovery in body rise, tori makes inside turn to shihonage, and throw extends as tori continues to back away from uke causing either a back fall or an elevated rolling break fall depending on the momentum and ukemi skill of uke.

7. Ushiro Ate

Same as in the 17, but lead in with the left foot and keep arms extended after throw.

8. Kote gaeshi

As uke attacks from ma-ai, tori breaks balance with a back step and outside push to uke's left front corner. On body rise recovery, tori flows into Kotegaeshi. As tori continues to move away to uke's inside, keeping at arms length, uke takes elevated rolling break fall. Tori continues to move until uke has landed.

125

9. Ushiro Kubi Gatame

Same as in #5, but as uke recovers in body rise, tori is on left foot and engages left hand by hooking the base of the thumb across uke's throat just under the jaw line while also stepping away from uke and maintaining control of uke's outstretched right arm. Uke submits and tori allows uke to back fall by releasing the neck lock and stepping away.

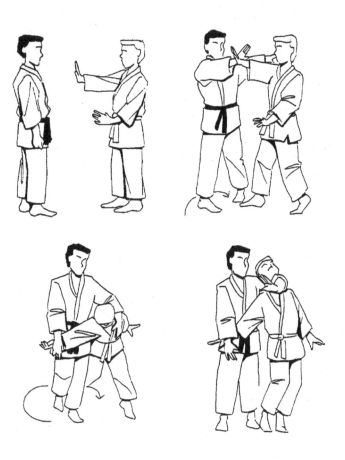

10. Shizumi Otoshi

As uke attacks, tori waits until uke has nearly made contact with tori's face, then drops directly down in a turning action to the right. Uke is prevented from completing the foot cycle of the step and does a rolling break fall over tori's body (some schools turn to the left in the drop and allow uke to take a preparatory step to the left for the roll -- both forms are acceptable).

V. A Note on the Koryu Katas

The Koryu Katas, or ancient style katas, are representative of the older forms of aiki from which the modern forms of Hanasu no kata, Ju Nana Hon Kata, and Owaza Ju Pon derive. The modern forms can be seen as the randori applications and in many cases the essential principled blue print for the techniques of these ancient ideas. As such, the Koryu are the roots for technical understanding and exploration of variations in application. Of the six Koryu kata, the most important for these ends are, Koryu Dai San Kata, Koryu Dai Yon Kata, Koryu Dai Go, and Koryu Dai Roku Kata. The study of these kata are usually undertaken from the rank of nidan on. San Kata and Yon Kata typically occupy our attention from nidan to yondan, while Go Kata and Roku Kata are typically the focus of godans and above. Since the scope of this book is intended to cover the material to go from white belt to shodan and since a complete technical description of the Koryu Katas would require a full textbook unto themselves to begin to do them justice, such a treatment will have to be pursued at a later date.

Ideas of Kata

I. Tori, Uke, and the Meaning of Kata

When we enter into the study of kata as a partnered exercise, a misunderstanding often arises that kata is in some way a peculiar form of combat simulation. Such an error is understandable since kata looks somewhat like combat and seems representative of conflict, but to consider kata in this way is to fundamentally miss the point.

So, what is the real meaning of kata? Kata, as we practice it, is **highly refined demonstration of principle that is repeated for the purpose of internalization.** As such, kata is a cooperative effort; wherein, both tori and uke are attempting to display, as clearly as possible, the workings of aikido principles in a dynamic forum. The purpose of kata and its practice lies in the fact that we train by repeating the same highly refined kata forms thousands of times. We practice this demonstration of principle over and over until it becomes internalized in our being.

At this point, the profound value of kata shows itself, for once you have internalized the central kata forms, then all the variations that occur in "combat scenarios" seem simplified, if not ridiculous, for their inefficiencies. Once you have spent the requisite number of repetitions training within highly efficient parameters of good kata, then the variations that arise are almost always of some less efficient variety and, as such, seem easier to handle.

This is not meant to disparage "combat simulation" as a training concept, and in our system we maintain the importance of training under stress and in resistive and quasi-competitive conditions in hand randori. To fully round out one's proficiency as a martial artist we know that such training is absolutely necessary, but we also maintain that a clear distinction and understanding of kata must be preserved so that we not confuse the purposes of the training regime.

129

Tori and uke are cooperative roles that are assumed for the sake of kata training. Uke's job is to give a clean and efficient committed attack as consistently as possible. Uke's next job is to recover balance, to regain a position for more attacks, and occasionally, to offer some form of prescribed resistance to tori, but this resistance is a far cry from uke's trying to thwart tori's every move. Again, we must take care that any particular resistance is implemented from the form of the kata; uke's strategies of attack and resistance are prescribed for a reason, and the reason is that those strategies and tactics have been found to be a useful training elements for both tori and uke to master.

Were we to fall into the combat simulation mode of kata training, we would quickly see a drastically reduced proficiency level in our aikidoka. As it stands now, both tori and uke practice good aikido principles -- same hand and foot, eye contact, ma-ai, center, unbendable arm, etc. Uke uses these principles as much as tori, but when uke devolves into a competitive, resistant, and deceptive role, then uke can no longer continue to maintain good aikido values, and as such uke will be cheated of the valuable benefits of the true internalization of off balance, efficient recovery, and skillful/viable resistance concepts. Instead, the combative uke will really be doing nothing more than enacting a control fantasy that is severely self-limiting to growth and understanding. Additionally, we should note that by allowing our practice of uke to degenerate, we are in fact cheating ourselves out of the opportunity to develop the proper "feel" for the techniques, for we know that if tori is doing his job right, he should "feel" nothing; it is uke who gets to feel the whole process of off balance, recovery, resistance, etc. In aikido systems where players mistakenly think that they must build techniques on the "feel" they get from being tori, we find an epidemic of rushed timing, techniques forced with strength, and cranking. All of these degenerated forms of practice can be directly attributed to the failure to understand the proper role and function of uke.

When you and your partner find trouble in your kata techniques, look first to uke, for over 90% of the time, the problem stems from a lack of legitimacy in attack. For tori to maintain integrity of principle, uke must maintain the integrity of attack. Uke is a demanding job because our doing it well requires the ability to both deliver a true and sound attack, coupled with a total giving up of control in off-balance. Uke must be the best complete aikido person he can be and still commit the attack, lose the balance, recover the balance, and re-attack. On a subconscious level, many people fear the feeling of being out of control in off balance, and subconsciously, they compensate for this fear by not really attacking. Once this problem is faced, and corrected, and uke can begin to deliver real attacks, then a whole new level becomes available to the aikidoka. Uke is a scary job, but its well worth the trouble to become the best uke you can be.

As a further note, we should consider that in our style of aikido, we do subject our kata to realistic testing, and that this testing is an ongoing and transformative process that has allowed us to maintain a high degree of confidence in our technical principles. Anyone who has come through our system and has serious and honest questions as to the viability of any technique is free to request that the technique in question be tested in a rigorous and realistic manner. In fact, over the past sixteen years, the standard forms of various kata techniques have changed, sometimes many times over. Tomiki's original twelve techniques became fifteen techniques and then became seventeen; the lines of off balance and the form and feel of joint locks and control positions have evolved, and as a result, the level of hand randori has increased dramatically. As the system grows and evolves, so does our understanding of it, and so techniques grow, change, and evolve into higher and higher forms. Such changes are never made for the sake of novelty but are simply changes that occur in the face of a clearer perception of truth.

II. Large and Small/Slow and Fast/Soft and Hard/Right and Wrong?

"slow is fast; fast is slow."
Musashi

As we progress in our aikido training, we often run up against many different ideas of how a given technique should be done. Commonly we begin to question if we might not be doing a given technique correctly or whether it would **really** work or not.

To gain a good perspective on these issues, it helps to consider that the techniques we are studying in kata form are not necessarily representative of their finished form. We must remember that the kata techniques are designed to train our bodies, minds, muscles, and nervous systems to respond to the stimulus of attack in certain principled ways. The techniques of the katas are not ends in themselves, but rather a means by which we condition our reflexes for optimal efficiency. Consequently, when we are attacked, our training will allow our automatic, reflexive system to respond and protect us. In effect, we will handle the problem of defending ourselves without even trying.

The katas are designed with this end in mind, and the way that the techniques are practiced reflect this goal. As we gain in aikido experience, we soon notice that various movements that we are practicing could be done in a smaller range of motion with smaller steps, tighter turns and circles, smaller wrist or arm actions, etc. At this point, by experimentation, we find that, often, the techniques seem to work better, easier, and more powerfully when executed in these smaller ways. It is wise to explore these variations, but as you progress in training, you must return to the standard, full sized range of motion. We practice these larger motions for two simple reasons. First, the large action is always easier to learn. Second, the large form contains the small form within it, but the small form only contains one element of the large movement. We have found that if a person trains exclusively in the application of small forms of techniques, when under certain conditions, whereby they must use the larger, fuller range of motion, they cannot automatically make the adjustment. Indeed, we find that under the influence of adrenaline, some people's actions tend to get shorter and smaller, so that, in effect, a regular size step becomes a small step, and a small step becomes no step at all. If this step is necessary for evasion, you can readily see the problem with always taking small steps in practice.

Please do not misunderstand, we are not doing kata with extra large steps or actions; we are simply taking the normal shoulder length steps and exploring our natural range of motion in our wrist and arm actions. For by practicing our aikido actions to the extent of our range of motions, we become adept at applying techniques throughout that range, but if we are conditioned to work in only a limited part of the range, and are then forced to deliver energy outside of this limited range, we lose our reflexive efficiency. Thus, we practice large to be able to work small.

A similar condition exists when we consider the issue of speed, for in practice of our katas, we work slowly, but in real life people attack at full speed. It would seem that we are making ourselves vulnerable by training at these slow speeds. Again, the reasons for training at slow speed are several. First, by training slowly, we increase the efficiency of our learning. Just as a person who is learning to play a musical instrument must begin slowly to master the proper actions and transitions before playing a song, so must the student slowly and accurately learn the proper movements and transitions before really being able to throw or control an attacker.

Next, speed effects cognition; by always working at a speed where you can perceive exactly what is happening in your own body and in your partner's, you build a profound sensitivity and awareness into your defensive structure. Once this sensitivity and awareness are in place, you will quickly find that the speed of the attacker becomes largely irrelevant to you. Whatever the speed, you will find that from your relaxed position at ma-ai, you can easily match the speed and let your subconscious defensive reflexes take over.

But the objection comes up, "Aren't some people so fast that you can't match their speed?" Well, not really, since from the defensive aikido concept, we find that if the attacker must cover the distance of standard ma-ai (hypothetically, let's say 6 feet), and you must evade the attack by a much smaller margin (say, 1 foot) over the same length of time; then you have a 6 to 1 advantage in time, which is to say that the attacker must be six times faster than you to exceed your defensive limits.

Additionally, the average speed of a person's center of gravity in motion in a combat situation rarely exceeds six to eight feet a second. Our normal training speed that we consider "slow" is four to six feet a second, so the gap is relatively small. Hand speed can reach up to 75 to 90 mph in a trained athlete (think of a pitcher throwing a fast ball), but the average person's hand speed is typically in the 65 to 80 mph range; again, the gap is not that great. Additionally, we must consider the speed of automatic reflex action vs. an action or attack that is directed by conscious thought. Here the gap in time grows very wide. We know that the subconscious can react in as little as one tenth of a second; whereas, the conscious mind (at its best) functions in one half second intervals. Consequently, against an attacker, who must by definition "decide" to attack and "decide" what to do next, we get a 4 to 1 advantage in time by using pure reflexive action.

Again, we train slowly so that we can train accurately. The great swordsman, Musashi once pointed out that "the sword that cuts fast, cuts nothing." But by learning our "cuts" slowly, we learn to hit our target with great consistency. To Musashi, speed was an illusion produced by the failure to "harmonize with the rhythm." By practicing slowly, we are able to "harmonize with the rhythm" of our partner with great consistency. Gradually, all sorts of rhythms, quick and slow, become familiar to us and we find that we are adept are blending no matter what the speed. Surprisingly, our slow motion practice is, in truth, the fastest way to develop accurate and efficient full speed self defense.

In the comparison of being hard or soft in our training, we find an amazing advantage by training strictly in softness. Of course, as we grow in skill and understanding so does our perception of softness, but basically, we can understand the concept of softness as an application of Jigoro Kano's great principle "maximum efficiency with minimum effort." In each technique, we strive to accomplish our goals by application of the minimum force possible. Naturally, when we begin our training, our use of force will be less than efficient and more than minimum. We tend toward the hard style because of misjudgment in timing and distance and small mistakes in principle coupled with the need to consciously direct our actions since they are not yet automatic and internalized. At this stage, we push too hard, we force techniques, and, while they still work, we find that they don't work easily.

As training progress over time, and we implement the principle of softness controlling hardness (ju yuko go sei-suru), we find ourselves growing consistently softer and softer. As actions become more automatic and principles become internalized, sensitivity to the attacker becomes a priority. Instead of trying to make the throw or establish the control technique, we focus on moving with the attacker's actions and reactions thereby exploiting and controlling the attacker's own voluntary and involuntary responses in a flowing manner (nagashi). This fluid nagashi mode feels magical, for at this stage, we find that we can effect throws and control techniques with only the lightest of touches, and with this soft touch, we can actually become more sensitive to what our partner's body is doing than our partner himself is.

Once we have come to this stage of complete softness, there is yet a further stage of application, which is to come to be able to actually switch from hard to soft and back instantly at will. To master this ability, we must be able to go quickly and absolutely from a full power feeling, to a fully relaxed state, in the blink of an eye, with completely appropriate timing and principle. This form of hardness is much different from the earlier form since this is hardness with proper principle to back it up joined by an almost cloud like softness. Great power comes from the ability to instantaneously transition from one to the other.

Finally, and perhaps most basically, we get down to issues of right and wrong. As we can see from the above, establishing clear parameters of what is right technically is difficult. Though we should

135

normally try to train with large, slow, soft actions, in application we occasionally find small, fast, hard actions, and both can be "right" depending on the circumstance.

Outside the "rightness" of employing the principles, in which we all make mistakes, there is no one right way to do aikido techniques. In fact, because we all make mistakes, it is perhaps easier to think of different applications as merely variations in "wrongness." Since no one can always embody the ideal principle of the art all the time, we are all some what equal in our own distinct wrongness. Some are more wrong than others, but none is absolutely right. By adopting this attitude, you will find it much easier to learn from different interpretations and variations in technique rather than be turned off by them because of the attitude of "who's right and who's wrong." We are all somewhat right and somewhat wrong, so explore all of it and grow.

III. Teacher's Variations and Student's Frustrations

Sometimes, we come across a student who complains that he or she is frustrated by the wide diversity of opinion from teacher to teacher on how certain techniques and katas are to be done. The fact is that opinions vary since in the process of learning aikido we all in some ways make aikido our own by adapting it to our own specific body types, temperament, rhythms, and ideas. The art is not a finite subject, but instead is an infinite object of study that grows with the inclusion of each new student and each new perspective.

The wise way to proceed is to not give in to the initial frustration that springs naturally from the desire for the one "best" way and to realize that all of your teachers and sempai are indeed sharing with you their own individual best way. These different views are fertile ground indeed, and it is in exploring these different ideas and how they relate back to fundamental principles that great technical growth can occur over a very short time. As Shihan Catherine Sullivan once pointed out, we are " in principles united, in artistry free." It may be that this freedom (frustrating though it may be) is the life blood of the art. In the end, rest assured that your teachers and sempai aren't playing some sort of cruel game on you; it is just that none of us should ever decide that we have fully understood any aspect of this art, for wherever we decide to become completely satisfied with our understanding, in that place, on that subject, we lose our perspective, we cease to apply critical examination, and we cease to grow.

Randori

"the true strategy of randori is to simply make order out of chaos."

Shihan Karl Geis

I. Some Thoughts on the Practice of Hand Randori

The practice of hand randori as a training concept dates back to early methods of training in the old style jujitsu ryu, particularly in the Kito Ryu, and Tenshin Shin'yo Ryu. These early forms of practice were called by various names; among the most notable are nokoi ai, ran ho, and midare geiko. The method of these practices centered around one partner making an attack and if the attack was weak or failed for some other reason, then it was countered; if the counter was weak, then it was countered, and so on.

The aim of such practices was to bring an air of realism back to the old style jujitsu forms that had grown theatrical and fake during the long period of peace brought about by the shogun, Tokogawa. The katas of these old styles had lost much of their sense of objective reality because they had not been tested with any rigor since the civil wars had ended. Evolutionarily, they had ceased competing, ceased adapting, and poor technical ideas were no longer being weeded out. The great old ryu's kata all began to devolve in terms of utility and slip more toward the aesthetic and spiritual paradigms. The common problem was first addressed by the sword schools, and by the late-19th century, kendo had revitalized kenjitsu forms by allowing for a means to realistically test its theories in shiai (competition). Kano's newly formed judo used randori and shiai for the same purpose. Kenji Tomiki, who had studied closely with both Kano and Ueshiba, realized that for an aikido system to remain grounded in reality, it also had to utilize a practice of randori. Shihan Karl Geis has described Mr. Tomiki's innovations toward this end in the following:

"Tomiki's contributions to the martial arts are numerous but two items stand out as perhaps the most significant. First, through a thorough understanding of countless aikido techniques (numbering in the thousands), he developed a few dozen basic techniques and new method of practice through which one could discover for oneself all the other variations. One might say that he developed the alphabet and grammar for aikido with which sentences of aikido may be written efficiently. Second, he developed a method which made possible the practice of randori and shiai without fear of injuries. Without randori . . . it is extremely difficult to develop a true fighting skill that is effective in defending oneself in a real life situation. Only a rare genius might master a realistic fighting art purely from kata practice or through pre-programmed actions and reactions; even such a genius would probably have to spend a long time developing a true fighting skill."

There is no doubt that learning toshu or hand randori is one of the most frustrating and trying aspects of aikido training. Yet, there is also no doubt that hand randori training is one of the most valuable and rewarding of practices. For in a very real sense, randori complements and completes the full aikido picture. Professor Tomiki has said as much.

"Randori practice is something that is done to give life to the real power of those techniques that were learned through kata. That is to say, randori provides the power to 'complete a painted dragon by filling in the eyes'."

The relationship between kata and randori is that each practice informs and shapes its counterpart. Were we to practice only kata,

139

we would have no objective means of testing our system or ourselves. Were we to only be concerned with randori, we would quickly lose sight of our fundamental principles. Kata gives us rules to follow, which we need, for as Mr. Tomiki once said, "a martial art without rules is mere violence," but the rules are empty without the realistic context that randori provides. Mr. Riki Kogure put it this way,

> "Kata without an understanding of the practicalities of randori is a meaningless dance, while randori without an understanding of the principles of kata techniques is not even Aikido."

Kata gives us theory; randori gives us practice; or perhaps even better, kata is our theoretical research lab, and randori is our proving ground. Kata constrains us safely within its rules and prescriptions, while randori confronts us with freedom and allows us to transcend our concepts and find the truth. Eventually, the practice of randori allows for the free, intuitive, and creative use of the internalized mechanisms and automatic responses that we have spent so much time and energy developing in kata. So far, so good.

Our frustration usually occurs when we find that when put under the stress of having to utilize our skills against someone of equal or greater skill level, in an unpredictable encounter, our techniques often fail. On the proving ground of randori, we get exposed to the little technical flaws that we didn't even suspect existed, and as stress increases, we find that we quickly forget basic principles, and much to our own chagrin, we become more competitive and more deceptive and more defensive, as our emotional self control becomes foiled.

Unfortunately, most randori players are not be able to count the number of times that they have come away from a randori session in confusion or frustration. All veteran randori players have experienced this process in themselves and have also observed it in almost every aikido player who has undertaken to study randori -- so

140

don't feel alone. This process is one that most of us have been through.

So how do we handle these frustrations? How do we turn this difficulty into advantage so that our study and practice of hand randori can take its rightful place in our training?

First, it is helpful to consider Shihan Karl Geis's advice to "transcend victory and defeat" (if you haven't read his **Book of Twelve Winds**, you should), for it is only by exploring the total picture that we arrive at real understanding. Mr. Tomiki also instructs us to make this transcendental leap by getting intimately familiar with defeat. We cannot achieve real success without understanding both sides of the equation, or as he put it, "in order to make clear the theory of victory, one must at the same time know the theory of defeat." So we must get rid of any idea of winning or losing, and instead concentrate on learning about the conditions that constitute victory and equally the conditions that constitute defeat.

Next, we should consider Jigoro Kano's instruction that randori is for training the mind, so that the mind and the technique become two sides of the same thing. Thought and action cease to be separated. We can begin to approach this unity by bringing our psychological state up to speed by abandoning preconceived ideas of attack and defense, and stopping the tendency to plan out our next move in advance. Instead, try to settle your mind like a still pool of water that reflects and responds to whatever passes before it with out any conscious design. This mind set is called mizu no kokoro and is a reflective form of Tomiki's "mushin" or no-mind and is also what Ueshiba called "becoming a mountain echo." These descriptions and names sounds esoteric, but what all these descriptions are pointing to is really just a mind set that is sensitive enough to what is going on to effectively respond in a completely automatic way. We become sensitive to our own bodily state and that of our partner's, and we become sensitive to any gaps or lapses, to itsuki (moments when our partner's intention stops) and are thereby ready to exploit any gap or lapse (kega no komyo). In order to be truly receptive to these momentary changes, we must train to control our own mind. These theories of mind go all the way back to the great zen warrior,

141

Musashi, who described the proper mindset for a martial artist as being your normal, everyday mind, unchanged by the situation of conflict remaining open, direct, centered and so relaxed that "the relaxation does not stop its relaxation for an instant." At first, such relaxed control seems impossible, but with practice and concentration, you can make it your standard practice.

Next, consider your posture. Staying in proper posture (shizen hon tai) is paramount, for only by keeping correct form can we remain completely open and responsive to the actions of our partner. Only by staying in shizen hon tai can we maintain relaxed freedom of movement. Tomiki saw a direct link between natural posture and natural mind (mushin/mugame, literally, no mind/no posture) and here again the great sword saint, Miaymoto Musashi instructs us that,

> "it is essential to make your natural bearing the
> bearing you use in the martial arts, and the
> bearing you use in the martial arts, your
> natural bearing."

What Musashi is telling us is to stay natural, don't get into any stance or particular posture but remain open and balanced. Keep your body in shizen hon tai with the weight on the balls of your feet, centered, relaxed, and natural.

Next, slow down -- way down -- until you begin to perceive **exactly** what is going on. Most people's randori suffers from this lack of basic perception. Stop worrying about the speed of realism, and just try to go as absolutely slow as you can force yourself to go. Such slow speed work helps to build awareness and sensitivity to the subtle changes that are always taking place both within our own bodies and in our partners. Always try to make this slow motion your baseline to work from, but always be willing and able to match the speed that your randori partner employs. Remember that speed is purely secondary to staying in harmony with the rhythm. Staying in the same rhythm and speed of your partner is essential, for if you don't learn to get consistently in the rhythm, you cannot learn to break or change the rhythm. This very slow, almost tai-chi speed, also seems impossible at first, but you can do it if you really apply yourself.

Next, relax and lighten up; try not to store any muscle tension in the hands, arms, or shoulders. Let your touch become soft and gentle, like holding a baby or petting a cat. When pushed on, yield and give way to the force without muscular resistance. This is the principle of ju (yielding) and nagashi (flowing).These principles are of utmost importance. Whenever we are connected to someone with our grasp we should strive to flow gently with the force, cooperate with it without any resistance and allow it to come to its natural conclusion in off balance. Here we are not trying to proactively destroy our partner's balance, but merely following the force they generate and discovering how it will ultimately undo its own structure.

Next, we must strive to only deliver energy to our partner using correct principle (center, same hand and foot, unbendable arm, posture, eye contact, and movement off the line). All of the physical power generated in randori should be the product of the movement or stillness of the whole body. This type of power is called hazumi (the force of momentum) and should never be confused with mere strength (ikioi). To implement hazumi, work from an attitude of absolute lightness, and never allow pressure to build up at the hands or wrists; never try to force a position or technique, and never resist with force or muscle. The power exerted upon our partner is generated by the whole body's momentum, yet it is transmitted through a light touch. This lightness of touch is essential to advanced randori since it allows us to feel our partner's movements, balance, rhythm, and tension. By touching lightly, we gain in sensitivity, and with greater sensitivity comes greater understanding and greater control.

Also, you must physically explore positions of off balance from the inside out. So, for awhile, make it easy for your partners to take you into off balance. In other words, open the window of opportunity to your partner and stop resisting basic balance breaks. To truly internalize randori, you must go through a stage where you have no resistance to off-balance at all. This stage allows you to internalize

143

the basic repetitive, pendulum like patterns that reoccur in randori. In this period of acting the perfectly cooperative uke, you give away your whole defensive structure so that you can develop an inside understanding of many vital aspects of off balance.

It is also helpful to get completely away from technique oriented thinking in your randori and focus entirely on just applying basic principles as cleanly as possible. Many people get stuck in their randori by focusing too narrowly on a given technique that they have had some success with. In judo, this is called the tokui waza (favorite technique), and over time we all develop them, but if we become satisfied with this technique and allow ourselves to constantly resort to it, we will be limiting our growth in other areas. To get out of this being stuck, you may find it useful to restrict yourself in the use of that technique for a given period, and instead try to just apply principles without any distinct idea of technique in mind. As the principles are applied, the techniques unfold naturally.

If you become too frustrated with yourself or your partner, it may be wise to stop free randori and instead work on some more structured randori drills and skill work; take turns and get completely away from the competitive feeling. You may often find it helpful to talk about the goals that you each have for your randori session before you begin so that you can help one another to achieve your individual goals. Sometimes, it is helpful to shift the focus to trying to help your partner to develop a technique on you rather than trying to ploy against him. In any case, try to foster a positive learning experience for both yourself and your partner. One way that higher grades can help when practicing randori with lower grades is by following the idea of mosukoshi (a little more), which means that if you are playing a nikyu then apply your techniques like an ikkyu; if playing a shodan, be a nidan. This idea of selective variability allows for a more enjoyable and educational randori since it asks the higher grade to try to play almost to their partner's level and deal with similar technical issues that are the focus of the lower grade's interest.

Finally, at some stage you must abandon any defensive concept of randori, for the heart of randori lies in offensive strategy. For the best results in our randori we must begin with practicing offensive tactics. This is due to the simple fact in order to learn true defensive skill, we must first come to understand the inner nature of offensive attack. We must learn what we need to learn from the inside out. Many people have a hard time with this idea since they believe that aikido is a purely defensive art. It may be more accurate to see aikido as about 95% defensive and 5% offensive, with randori being the primary offensive focus. It is only natural to be on the defense when you start to learn randori, but you soon find that being on the offensive, is the real key to growth and understanding in randori, for it is only by fully embodying the attack that we can ever find our way toward understanding what it means to harmonize and flow with the attack. We must not retreat into mere defensiveness. Of course, we all slip into the defensive mind occasionally. But the problem comes when defense displaces offense in our practice as a regular matter of course.

This is not a new phenomena in the world of the martial arts; the same was true in Musashi's day. The zen swordsman observed that most warriors of his time practiced and studied defense to such a degree that they lost their Way, and that because of this they ended up being manipulated and forced out of control by their opponents. Offensive strategy and mindset, stalking like a predator, and training to attack and overcome in a direct and straightforward way were the keystones of Musashi's proven method. Just as in Musashi's time, if you approach randori with a defensive mind, you will only become more frustrated, out maneuvered and manipulated. We must become somewhat predatory to excel at randori. By attacking we undertake risk, but without risk, there is little growth, so cast caution to the wind, and attack.

As we advance in our study of randori, one important practice to integrate into our behavior is the elimination of all arbitrary actions, whether great or small, (in Musashi's words, "Do nothing that is useless"). Once we come to recognize our tendency to commit to sequences of action or to movements with no real intention, we can begin to learn to control our bodily processes to a much finer degree. For awhile, this task of elimination can seem impossible, but by consistent application and awareness, we can in fact learn to "drive our bodies" much like we drive our cars. When we learn to drive, we all go through an awkward, conscious effort phase of controlling the actions of our automobile. Eventually, with persistence and some luck, we survive this phase and learn to operate our vehicles without any arbitrary actions in a completely automatic and safe way. At first, it may seem strange that we have to follow a similar process with our bodies; however, to develop fine motor control, sensitivity, and reflexive response requires the same type of conscious effort.

Once we have gained some skill at controlling our own body and mind, then we can begin to apply ourselves to the control and manipulation of our partner's body. Again, we must proceed with conscious effort, work slowly and softly, in much the same way we learn to play a musical instrument. Gradually, as we become more and more familiar with the way that the instrument responds to our actions, we can begin to evolve from making noise into making music. We begin to "play" our partner's balance, reflex actions, and even intentions with our actions in a rhythmic and flowing manner. What begins as a struggle transforms into an effortless and harmonious interaction of complex forces and variables that our intuitive mind creatively plays with. If we have ever experienced this level of randori, then we know with certainty, the absolute power of aiki.

Sokaku Takeda, the sensei who taught Daito Ryu aikijujitsu to Ueshiba, once remarked that the true power of aiki was the ability to defeat your opponent with a mere glance. This high stage of randori reveals such a possibility and opens the way for the student to actually achieve this potential.

We should remember that in randori, as well as in kata, we always try to train to principled reactions and never let our randori or kata devolve into specific " if he does this, you do that" form of reaction training. Such training is popular in jujitsu, but in aikido we always strive to build reactions that resort back to fundamental principles and allow the specific techniques to manifest as the side effect of pure principle. The effect of such training in randori is that given techniques arise from the foundation of principle in a spontaneous, intuitive, and creative way. Going far beyond simple automatic reflex responses, at this stage, the aikidoka functions without concept or design and is more at play with his partner, rather than working against his adversary.

Gone are all concepts of effecting or manipulating the partner's balance or reflexes, and all that is left is a sense of moment to moment flowing awareness. Yet again, this sounds esoteric, but the simple fact is that words do not do justice to this state of high level randori play, for the awareness goes beyond one's own body and beyond sensitivity of the partner's body and forms a gestalt -- a whole that is greater than the sum of its parts-- and it is from this, "greater whole," that the creative, playful, and effortless aikido comes.

II. Exercises and Drills to Develop Randori

These exercises and drills are not in any way a replacement of kata. The primary skills of randori are all developed through repetitious kata training. These exercises are only useful as supplements to the standard training. Many of them can help develop what Tomiki called nagashi no ri (principle of flowing) that he described as "flowing with a force you have grasped and with which you cooperate."

Free Hand to the Face Drill -- have your partner cover your hands, then randomly release a hand, you try to move the freed hand instantly to your partner's face.

Sticky Hands -- have your partner move hands and body in random manner as you try to stick to the hands with a light touch.

Palm to Palm -- take up a cross side position with your partner and extend hands out palm to palm. Advance in pushing action with tsugiashi keeping the palm to palm position. Work back and forth

147

trying to maintain the same pressure between the hands, never letting it build up or diminish. Take turns leading the action.

Hand Changes -- Work lightly back and forth with a variety of hand change combinations in a flowing manner.
    1) The underhand pass from shomen ate
    2) Tenkai kote hineri to kote gaeshi and back
    3) Inside butterfly pick up to kote gaeshi
    4) Hineri to waki gatame to kote gaeshi to kote mawashi
    5) Center line pass -- never try to control by reaching across your own center line. Once the hand becomes uncomfortable in any control position, it is time to change hands.

Polishing the Mirror and Writing Your Name – with hands kept always in center and using only the actions of the legs (as we do in the final movement of the Walking kata), attempt to write your name in cursive in the air. Start small and work larger until you work through the full range of motion of your knees. Maintain your posture and centering. Then, with a partner facing you in contact with your hands, repeat the same exercise, taking turns writing and following the action. Begin moving side to side, as if writing on a large blackboard. Next, repeat the exercise in a circular manner, as if writing on the inside of a cylinder with your partner on the outside. Next, take up a position perpendicular to your partner's arms, as in a standard balance break in the Seventeen, and write and follow. This exercise trains us to move and follow in random and unpredictable ways while maintaining strict principles of center; consequently, it is vital that we do not allow our arms to move independently in order to compensate for errors that we make in our leg actions. In other words, keep your unbendable arms and center throughout the drill.

Following Behind the Arm – with unbendable arm and center, practice following your partner's forward and backward turning actions from a position behind his arm. Do not attempt to turn your partner, only follow and allow his actions to turn you. Float in this control position, and if your partner turns too far for you to maintain the position, simply change sides and float behind his other arm.

Follow the Force – have your partner push and pull you in random ways. First, follow the random actions and turn naturally with the force, keeping center and unbendable arm, while extending your step slightly. Next, as your partner pushes or pulls, follow the action and introduce a perpendicular off balance up or down. Finally, have your partner attempt to gently force a technique on you, follow and turn and allow yourself to close your hand and grasp his wrist when the position naturally occurs.

Holding Out of Center – have your partner move one hand out of center and practice centering on the hand with unbendable arm to hold him in his out of center condition. Use only the mirror side hand and keep the second hand free to prevent him from closing on you. Any force that your partner exerts in this weak structure will compress him and force him onto one foot.

Static Locks and Counters -- work from any particular lock position-- stop and identify the lines of force employed in the lock. Move with the lines into counter position or release. An excellent example of this is to experiment with applying a perpendicular line of force to your partner once you have been put into a spine lock from shomen-ate. Another is to work from being held in double kotegaeshi (wrist locks on both hands), and as your partner tries to make the technique on one side, you use the opposite hand to pull or push perpendicularly.

Release Variations -- An advanced randori man, Shihan Dennis Doris, once stated that you don't get great randori by doing thousands of hours randori; you get great randori by doing thousands of hours of releases. With this in mind, we can see that it might be wise to explore all manner of variations of releases. Have your partner attack with different grips, from different angles, use one hand or two, have uke use active attacks by pushing or pulling once he has grasped, try static releases, use tension and compression, try releases that expand the distance and stretch the attacker out, or that contract the distance and shorten the attack.

Active Releases -- turn releases into active gripping techniques -- as uke begins to grab your wrist, you move as in a release and grasp uke instead. The release action is identical except that tori has grasped uke.

Walking Off-balance -- as uke walks, you walk in rhythm beside him with your arm lightly draped around the shoulder. On uke's forward step, you cause extension as lightly as you can. The extension comes from the incremental lengthening of your step, not the push of the arm. Next, in the same manner, while walking, retard uke's shoulder as lightly as possible to cause off balance. The goal here is for uke to feel nothing except the off balance. The off balance is a product of the subtle change in rhythm, either by shortening or lengthening of your step in a minute and incremental way.

Static Off- Balance -- Do this as lightly as possible, touching hands or wrist in any manner. Have uke shift the weight on his feet without stepping -- forward, back, side to side, etc., and you mirror this action and extend it as lightly as possible into off balance. Don't lead uke, only follow, and keep it as slow and light as you can.

One Step Off-Balance -- This practice is an extension of the above exercise, but have uke begin to take a step. Work the off balance on the weight shift that tends to precede the step and work on extensions of the step itself with mirrored actions. Again, do this drill as lightly as you can, as slowly as you can, always following, not leading.

Asymmetrical Stepping -- Same as above but instead of mirroring the step, begin to become asymmetrical to uke. If uke steps little, you step big. If uke steps big, you step bigger, or away, or little, or stop. As uke steps right, you go left. As uke steps right, you step perpendicular to the line back or forward. Use steps, hip switches,

150

and goblet steps to create asymmetry with uke. This is also a form of off balance produced by altering rhythm.

Asymmetrical Tension – from a static position, have your partner push with both arms on your chest while you attempt to collapse his arms by grasping his collars and curling. This is a symmetrical tension and is stable. Next, while under this tension suddenly release one hand, thus producing an asymmetrical and unstable structure and your partner's arms collapse as he goes off balance. This drill is a demonstration of a profound structural principle that can be applied in a wide variety of ways including hand changes and sudden wrist reversals wherein a tension is set up in one side of your partner's body, suddenly released, and simultaneously reinitiated in the opposite side.

Multiple attack training -- Training against multiple opponents is one of the most dynamic and impressive forms of aikido training. Unfortunately, it is also one of the most dangerous. Still, given mature and reasonable participants, it is possible to train against multiple opponents without injury.

The benefits of such training include: developing the ability to respond to attacks from all directions, learning valuable strategies of evasion and control, learning the importance of constant movement, and the building up of the consistent flowing awareness and subconscious adjustment to the rapidly changing flow of events.

We have a wide spectrum of ways to proceed in multiple attack training spanning from the most controlled to the most chaotic. Obviously, the more slow and controlled you can keep it, the less dangerous the training will be. For safety's sake, you should first work with very controlled exercises: have your partners attack one at a time, limit the forms of attack used, work in slow motion, and focus primarily on evasion and movement.

Over several years, as experience builds, your multiple attack training can develop -- always within the bounds of safety -- until you are dealing with simultaneously occurring attacks, coming at

151

you from all angles, executed at full speed, and to which you respond with full throws and locks. In essence, you will basically be playing full out randori with several persons at once. Take note, this level of play is **extremely dangerous** and requires extraordinarily mature uke's and great self control in order to prevent serious injury. In fact, it is suggested that this completely chaotic level of multiple attack training is so dangerous that it should never be attempted by anyone below the rank and skill level of yondan, for the chances of injury are just too high.

III. Tanto Randori and Shiai

> "Tanto randori, like most sports, by its rules and
> nature predicts that the strongest and most
> athletic person will prevail; hardly a viable idea if
> we are to develop an Aikido form that is useful
> and productive to all who practice, large or small,
> strong or weak."
>
> Shihan Karl Geis

This discussion of randori would be incomplete if it did not include a few thoughts on the subject of knife randori and shiai.

First of all, in our system of Aikido training, we use and preserve tanto randori as a supplement to our hand randori training. We use tanto work to stress issues of evasion, timing, and counter attack, and we attempt at all times to work within a reality framework (i.e. we treat the tanto like it is a real weapon, rather than a piece of sports equipment used to score points with or against). In other words, we practice knife randori as a survival based skill, not as a competitive sport.

The shiai (competition) aspect of knife randori that Professor Tomiki developed and that has been carried on by Mr. Ohba and his successor, Mr. Nariyama of the Japan Aikido Association, take tanto randori into a rule based, competitive sport, and like most competitive sports, we can see that its practice is most suitable for young, strong, quick athletes who are good at learning and following the rules. It is completely appropriate for the Japanese players to practice in this way, if they wish, simply because in Japan they live in a society that presents them with a low probability of being assaulted by some one with a real knife.

We should also consider, that the average competitive Japanese Aikido player is a college athlete in his late teens or early twenties, but in this country, the average age of an Aikido student is between 30 and 45. In Japan, we find a low incidence of violent crime; while in this country, we are faced with a very high incidence violence; consequently, we must train in such a way that takes these issues and differences into account. Obviously, such differences must influence our training goals and values, and even our mind set, for in real self defense situations there is a tremendous risk that goes along with the idea of "trying to win," and in real conflicts you stand a much better chance if you simply "try not to lose." These two concepts may seem the same, but rest assured that the difference between them can mean the difference between life and death.

There is nothing principally wrong with competitive aikido training and sport application, and it is easy to understand why Mr. Tomiki implemented the sport system, as a valuable means of objective measurement and skill assessment. Students should rest assured that there is much to be gleaned from such study and training; however, at this time, in this period of history, and in this society, we cannot in good conscience teach skills or practice skills that do not afford the benefits of realistic self defense and self protection for middle aged persons living in a dangerously violent society.

In our system of Aikido training, if the smallest cannot overcome the largest, and the weakest prevail over the strongest with any given technique (or form of training), then that technique is either modified or discarded as unsuitable for reality. By turning aside from both the aesthetic and athletic criteria for success, we have developed a uniquely realistic form of aikido training that fosters a true and abiding sense of self confidence and security by maintaining real parameters of self defense using proper principle and mind set.

IV. Forms of Off Balance --Kuzure no Jotai

Like it or not, we spend a considerable amount of our life in states of off balance and recovery from off balance, from the subtleties of the weight shifting from our heel to our little toes to the obvious and sometimes painful tipping back too far in our chair. Aikido katas and randori practice provide us an intensive laboratory in which to carefully study and eventually understand
the cycle of balance to off-balance to recovery of balance, and the general state of being called disequalibrium.

In the beginning, we naturally treat off balance in ourselves like some kind of monster. We're afraid of it and we try to avoid it. But as our aikido training matures, we find ourselves befriending this monster; we get to know it, and we get familiar with its ways. We end up actually enjoying the off balance monster's company. Eventually, we recognize that this monster has become our teacher, and we study it at every opportunity, for now we know that to truly understand off balance in others, we must first understand it in ourselves. Here are a few observations on this all to common, but little understood condition.

1. Ball of foot (big toe) -- Heel -- Little toe cycle
This cycle of balance and off-balance concerns the way our body weight shifts on a given foot. If we examine the structure of a foot carefully, we find that it is basically a triangle defined by the big toe, heel, and little toe. Our maximum stability occurs when our weight is centered on the ball of the foot, largely behind the big toe, as our weight shifts to our heel, the knee straightens and off balance occurs to the rear. As we pitch forward in response to this, our weight often shifts to the outside edge of our foot and our little toe, and we are off balance to the front corner. Learning to control and respond to these little shifts in weight, both in ourselves and in others, broadens our understanding of off balance.

2. Parallel and perpendicular lines

As we consider the lines of off balance, we will notice that our primary weaknesses occur in the lines that are parallel to the line of our feet or line of travel and perpendicular to the line of our feet or line of travel. In other words, if as we step we are subjected to a force that draws us further than we intended to step (parallel) or intersects our line at right angles (perpendicular) thereby interrupting our step, we go off-balance. These two basic lines can be used to effect off balance both forward and backward.

3. Body rise and Body drop

As we discussed in the physical principles section, we find that the center of gravity rises and falls in every foot cycle. When the feet are apart we are in body drop, and when the feet are together, we are in body rise. This natural rising and falling rhythm can be exploited to create off balance by first matching or mirroring exactly your partners rhythm of rise and fall and then extending the body action slightly to amplify the effect or by simply holding the person at the peak of his rise or bottom of his drop. This kuzushi is akin to toppling a person off a high cliff or holding down a person who is stuck in a hole.

4. Tension and compression

Tension and compression refers to the condition of storing mechanical energy in the physical system and then suddenly releasing it, like the recoil of a spring that is stretched and released or compressed and released. For example, this concept can be utilized to effect off balance when your partner attempts to immobilize you with a strong grip on your arm. You respond by relaxing the arm and stepping slightly away from his center. Since the arm is relaxed, it acts as an efficient transmission of the force exerted by the step thus creating a pulling tension. This pull must come from the step and not from the arm itself, to have its maximum effect. Once proper tension is effected, you release the tension suddenly by reversing direction and your partner must now try to compensate for the force he has been exerting; his own stored energy comes back to haunt him, and he goes off balance. Of course the process can also be reversed; in

155

this case, you create compression by loading part of your body weight on your partner, so that he is actually holding part of your weight up, and then suddenly release the compression (by putting the weight onto your own foot) thus effecting off-balance. Tension/compression kuzushi can be done with foot pounds of pressure or mere micro ounces.

5. The body's inability to efficiently respond to two differing lines of force -- the advantage of curves over straight lines
Interestingly, the human body only responds well to one line of force acting on it at a time. Because of this fact, the body is subject to off balance when it is forced to try to respond to and compensate for more than one force acting upon it at one time. In effect, we are only strong in one plane at a time; this is why we don't see people walking around while they do weight lifting exercises, and in fact, if they were forced to step or walk while lifting a heavy weight, the results could be quite catastrophic. The knowledge of this human weakness can be used to create off balance in a number of ways. For instance, in randori you may load weight on your partner with one hand while the other hand effects a push on your partner's perpendicular line. Your partner's nervous system is now caught on the horns of the off balance dilemma since he can only effectively compensate for one of the attacking forces. Incidentally, this is why a curved attack, a line of force that describes an arc, is more difficult to adjust to or compensate for. For example, as you begin a push, allow your hand and body action to define an arc so that the push ends with the hand withdrawing slightly. As your partner's body responds to the line of force of the push, your natural withdrawal exploits his compensation. Should your center drop subtly as this change occurs, your partner will be forced to deal with not only two lines of force, but three. Faced with the convergence of three forces at once, off balance occurs.

6. Hando no Kuzushi -- the pendulum like quality of recovery
Hando no kuzushi is typically described as breaking the balance in one direction in order to throw in the opposite direction.

156

Conceptually, it is very similar to tension and compression, but this form of off balance depends primarily on the pendulum like quality of the recovery of balance. When we go off balance in a certain direction, our body fights to control and achieve homeostasis i.e. recover balance. But, the effort to come back on balance is itself subject to off balance and the compensatory reaction often over shoots its mark, so that off balance shifts from one corner to the opposite corner. Should we be pulled to our front right, our own resistance to the pull makes us vulnerable to our back left. The weight of the body swings like the pendulum of an old grandfather clock, and as we try to get back to balance, our very effort puts our balance more in jeopardy. As the cycle continues and the center of gravity swings back and forth, the oscillation degenerates and balance is lost.

7. Interruption of intent or concentration
Off balance can occur any time our intention is interrupted. This intent may be conscious or unconscious. Consciously, if you intend to grab your partner's hand and just as you attempt to do so, his hand moves out of range, your natural tracking of the target will take you off balance. Unconsciously, should you begin to step but find that you are not allowed to put your foot down where it would naturally fall, where your foot unconsciously aimed, the shortening or lengthening of the step can produce off balance. This concept also applies to anything that suddenly breaks your concentration (called shishin, stop the mind), a sudden gesture, or sound; at the right moment, even something as innocuous as a raised eyebrow can lead to off balance. Should you break your own concentration, for instance by trying to speak, or by shifting from unconscious flowing reaction to conscious thinking, your balance may go in jeopardy. Should you feel unconsciously threatened, your concentration may be broken. Any of these actions may cause off balance in themselves or facilitate a more physical disruption of balance simultaneously.

8. Physiology of hands, eyes, and breath

Understanding the subtle ways in which our hands, eyes, and breath effect our muscular structure can prove very fruitful in the study of off balance. Generally speaking, when our hands are palm up, we are curling and primarily engaging the muscles of the front of our body, and palm down we are pushing and engaging the muscles of back of our body. When the palms turn up, we are vulnerable backward; when palms turn down, forward. If we close our eyes suddenly, we pitch forward; if we open them suddenly, raising the eyebrows, we pitch back. If we breathe out quickly, we shift forward; breathe in quickly, we shift back. All such patterns of actions have a direct bearing on controlling off balance.

9. Ideas of tsukuri before kuzushi -- preparing the self and other
Typically we consider that in the three elements of a throw, kuzushi (balance break), tsukuri (fitting and preparation),and kake (execution), that we begin with kuzushi. However, as we refine our ideas of creating kuzushi we find that before effecting off balance, we should implement tsukuri. Tomiki described this clearly as consisting of two elements: the tsukuri of preparing the self and the tsukuri of preparing the opponent. By preparing the self, we must include elements such as obtaining posture (shizen hon tai), unbendable arm (tegatana), and eye contact (metsuke). Also as we prepare ourselves we may include the transition from normal stepping (ayumi ashi) into following stepping (tsugi ashi). Ideally, all of these changes are achieved before ma-ai is reached. In the tsukuri of preparing the opponent, we find elements of taking control of the opponent by controlling the space and distance between you. If possible you want to begin reacting to your opponent from what has been called a "pre-ma-ai" ma-ai of up to eighteen feet away. At ma-ai you complete the preparing of the opponent by implementing evasion, which protects you, and kuzushi, which prepares the opponent to become subject to the technique. His responses and attempts to recover and launch secondary attacks open him up to further tsukuri and further kuzushi until he becomes so unstable that the technique or fall occurs naturally as the byproduct of the ever increasing inefficiency of the responses.

Being a Student and Being a Teacher

I. Positive Attitudes in Training for Aikido

"If you have a wide knowledge of the ways, you encounter them in everything ... it is essential for each of us to cultivate and polish our individual path."

Musashi

There are a number of attitudes, ideas, philosophies and ethical principles that help us to progress in our aikido training. Two of the most central are Jigoro Kano's philosophies of "maximum efficiency with minimum effort" and his admonition to always practice in a spirit of "mutual welfare and benefit." Additionally, the principle of intellectual honesty is crucial to the study of this art, and we must abandon all falsehood of mind and keep our training as pure and straight as possible. We should never cling to our false opinions, and always be ready to open up and receive the truth.

As we become more absorbed with the art, a spirit of wholehearted commitment overtakes us, and this spirit becomes active in all areas of our lives and grants us the capacity to act and react in completely committed ways, without self-doubt or hesitation.

Aikido also teaches us about balance in life, both internally and externally. We must always strive for a dynamic and ever changing sense of balance both within our center of gravity and in the center of our being. Balance is of utmost value both in our physical body and in our character.

Aikido also helps us to define our boundaries in life more clearly and teaches us not to be defeated by defeat, for through the wisdom of aikido, we turn every defeat into an opportunity to find a new perspective.

Through the operative principles of blending, yielding, turning, flowing, and following, we can develop profound interpersonal strategies for conflicts on all levels, physical, mental, or emotional.

Finally, aikido allows us the opportunity to embrace and accomplish true mastery in life: to saturate ourselves so thoroughly and completely, to internalize principle, and to open ourselves up to the real power that lies potentially within us all. Once, as a young sandan, the author asked Shihan Harry Wright, who at the time seemed technically light-years ahead of him, what the big technical secret was, how could he so easily toy with him in randori? What was he missing? Harry just grinned and said, "Time. That's all. It just takes time. That's where the magic comes from. You just keep going and practicing and doing it, and eventually, it just becomes like this."

Shihan Karl Geis has said much the same when he would tell white belts that the only difference between themselves and sixth degree black belts is "time and ethics." If you practice long enough, you are going to get there, and as long as you continue to strive toward acting out of sound ethical principle, you will find that true mastery in your life is an actual possibility because the system will nourish and embrace you freely. So, go forward and achieve mastery in your life, and whatever you do or wherever you go you will stand on a truly solid foundation for life.

II. Teaching Aikido

The longer we are in aikido, the more it becomes apparent that to really progress, we must not only become highly proficient in the techniques but must also become teachers of this fine art. Indeed teaching is a requirement for higher dan grades, yet few of us feel completely confident in our ability as teachers all the time. Perhaps, our difficulty sometimes stems from the fact that aikido is multi-faceted, and to really teach it requires that we not only deal with matters of education (imparting knowledge), but also of internalization (honing skills), and finally of character (developing ethics).

Much of what this book has been about technically has been the internalization of the physical and psychological acts that make aikido work. Internalization deals with **how** aikido functions, with automatic, precise reflex action. Education gives us **why** aikido works. A true educator knows that for anybody to do anything well, they need to understand why they are doing what they are doing. Too often in the world of the martial arts, there has been a tendency for teachers to just monkey-see monkey-do their way through, giving students a visual picture to work from and little if any rationale. Such teaching is better than nothing and is even very understandable given the usual existence of a language barrier between Asian teachers and western students. But the problem comes when the western teachers adopts this form of teaching with their own students -- they are imitating the Asian teacher's style of teaching, but in doing so, the misguided attempt to maintain tradition becomes the perpetuation of inefficient teaching methods. To compound this problem, we find numerous martial art systems wherein the only rationale given for why something is done in a particular way is that "Great Master So-In-So" did it that way, and so we must do it that way too. You can readily see that such teaching styles and rationales are not at all adequate for the purposes of true education.

To develop our educational sense as teachers of aikido, we must strive to give our students the best that we have and to always seek to help them surpass us. As we teach aikido, it is wise to maintain the perspective that we are in fact involved with an ongoing project of quality control, experimentation, and explanation applied to both ourselves and our students. With this in mind, the following are a few ideas that apply the concepts of quality control and educational awareness to the process of teaching aikido:

1. The moment we become satisfied that we really fully understand something, is the moment that we cease to grow in understanding of that object. We cannot afford to become self satisfied about any aspect of aikido. As teachers we must strive for continuous growth and improvement of ourselves, for if we do not continue to grow in knowledge and skill, then we will find that we have little to teach.

2. Abandon your deep inner need to compete with those around you. Develop a cooperative mind-set so that you no longer are in competition with your peers. Instead of trying to be better than anyone else, find out how to learn from everyone else. In this way, everybody wins. A true teacher's actions benefit both himself and the student, but the goal remains to elevate the student beyond the teacher's own level of skill or insight.

3. Keep an eye on fundamentals, principles, and technical correctness. Since it takes just as long to train someone poorly as it does to train someone to do something well, make sure you don't waste time by showing an incorrect way to do something. Be technically strict with your self.

4. Abandon perfection as an unrealistic and self defeating strategy. Work with the concept of ever increasing quality as the goal, not perfection. A goal of perfection is self destructive in its impossibility, but continuous improvement in all skills and activities is possible and positive.

5. Try to act as a leader, to inspire and lead the direction as a positive model to work from. Avoid being a negative supervisor, who is there to catch the student's mistakes. We must always strive to become a positive influence on the student rather than a negative or oppressive influence.

6. Break down the barrier to teaching by being yourself. Don't make teaching into an act. Don't be too dogmatic, too "teachy or preachy." Never talk down to students or in any way diminish the student's self respect. Rather, treat them as an equal who you happen to be helping, not as some sort of pathetic fool who is dependent on your help and wisdom. We must strive to empower the student, not elevate our own egos as teachers. We must attempt to eliminate our student's fear and develop trust. Even when we must confront problems or chastise a student for unacceptable behavior, though we do so directly, we do it without anger or malice.

7. We should not rely on simplistic explanations or easy answers, but rather develop our technical vocabulary and our means of demonstrating principle and descriptive analogies for techniques. For example, don't just use the principle term "unbendable arm," but

define what that is for the beginning student. Be able to explain not only how things are done but why they are done. Imagine you are teaching to a blind student and must describe and explain the techniques (that you usually just demonstrate physically) with language.

8. Remember that change that is slow is change that sticks. Remain aware of the amount of time it takes to internalize and really own the art of aikido. Don't push students too fast, but allow each to go at his or her own pace. Pressure need not be applied. The work must remain joyful with each student achieving positive successes and accomplishing their individual goals in their own time.

9. Transform the teaching relationship into friendship -- establish genuine positive regard for the student as a fellow aikidoka and as a human being. If you care about your students, and they know you care, you have already won the battle.

10. Remember that our first duty as teachers is to ask ourselves how we can provide the highest quality aikido education possible so that our students will receive the maximum benefits of skill, knowledge, and personal development in the shortest amount of time. From this standpoint, we are indeed involved in creating and monitoring a quality controlled educational system, not built for the glorification of the hierarchy, for the sensei's ego, to make a fast buck, or for any other reason, but for the elevation of knowledge and the benefit of the student.

11. As teachers, we must foster an environment of positive reinforcement, continuous improvement, and achievement for our students. For example, when making corrections, don't point out what's wrong, but begin with what is right and add to it to make it better:

Not : " No, that was wrong. You didn't keep eye contact."

Not: "That was a good technique, **but** you need to keep eye contact etc."

But Rather: " That's really good, now lets make it even better. Try keeping eye contact and see if you can tell a difference."

The first example is completely negative, while the second starts out positive then negates itself by using the word "but." Watch out for this all too common negative teaching habit.

12. Try to make a point of returning to principles and showing how different techniques are all just differing applications of the same few rules and principles. Describe not only how to do the mechanics of a given technique but also how it feels when the technique is right so that the student can learn to feel for the sweet spot.

13. For any given lesson time, pick one thing to focus on and correct, or build and repeat, and stick to it. Too often, students are overwhelmed by too much input at once; too much technical data overloads the student's ability integrate, understand, and utilize the information. Too much help can impair learning.

14. Always try to foster tolerance for technical variations that come up, as long as they are safe for practice and within principle. The large variety of ways to do techniques is confusing and uncomfortable to some students. Help them to develop a tolerance for variations in the system, and let them know that as they become real artists and teachers, they will also have their own unique way of doing things.

15. Make sure that you teach not only tori skills but uke skills as well. In other words, don't just focus on tori's throw or lock but make sure that good aikido principles are also being applied to uke. Uke should be the best aikidoka he can be, even while attacking and falling. By building better uke's, we build better tori's, and the whole process upgrades.

16. Since personal affirmation is one of the most powerful educational tools, and since it has the added value of helping to foster self confidence and self esteem, it is critical that we as teachers try to empower and affirm our students daily. Learn each student's name, and use the name often. Listen to what students have to say,

and include them when possible in conversations. Avoid the tendency to settle into cliques, and don't play favorites with your time and attention. Give genuine and generous praise for student's accomplishments -- in short, treat them as you would wish them to treat you.

17. It is important that we as teachers keep the practice light-hearted and fun. Having fun and being entertained are some of the most overlooked, yet potent, educational tools at our disposal. This is not to suggest that we become entertainers and put on shows for students, but rather that we use fun as the amazing motivational force that it can be; so have fun with your practice and with your with students.

18. Ultimately, the true heart of the matter is this – our students do not really care what we know, or how much we know, how good we are, or what rank we hold – all that really matters is in the final analysis is that we as teachers care about them, and that they know we care. The rest will take care of itself.

19. The teacher must always keep a close check on his own ego, for there is a grave price to be paid for self glorification in the martial arts, and the same was true in Musashi's day. He writes, "The martial arts are rife with flamboyant showmanship and commercialization on the part of both students and teachers; the result of this amateurism can only be serious wounds." If we opt for the path of the amateur and do not seek to become truly professional in our teaching, then we too are in for serious wounds. To achieve this level of professionalism requires far more than mere time on the mat and knowledge of aikido. It requires the development of skills and knowledge in areas such as education, psychology, public speaking, exercise physiology and biomechanics, physics, organizational psychology, classroom management, and of course philosophy and history. To become well rounded in all these areas is a daunting challenge that may require a life time, but in the end, such studies are the requirement for truly becoming a great professional teacher.

20. Professor Tomiki said that the goal of a true educator is to teach in a rational and objective way, so that out of one hundred

students, all can make progress when they try. This is a much higher goal than trying to turn one or two students into geniuses. The aim of education should be for the benefit of all.

It is the author's hope that some of these points will help you in your teaching, for in a real sense, the teacher of aikido is responsible for aikido's future. Who can say what the future will bring? The best we can do is build as strong a foundation as possible in the present, develop ourselves and our art to the highest standards possible, and pass on all that we have to the future generations of aikidoka.

*Nothing is so strong as gentleness,
and nothing so gentle as true
strength.*

Aikido and Spirituality

"true budo is love."
Ueshiba, founder of aikido

"mutual welfare and benefit"
Kano, founder of judo

There are many aikido books that address the spiritual dimensions of aikido. This book is one of the few that has mostly avoided the subject, but we would be remiss if we did not at least give a glance toward aikido as a spiritual practice and spiritual reality.

Spirituality intersects aikido in two primary ways. First, because the founder of the art was a man of pre-modern out look and had little in the way of scientific education, Ueshiba was forced to resort to explaining his art through the lens of his religious beliefs. We cannot blame him, for he was using the most sophisticated concepts and language that he had. His art dovetailed with his faith and through a process of deep intuitive genius became real and consistent within its own framework. However, to really understand the founder's explanations of his art, required that his pupils study and practice Shinto religion. Ueshiba knew it worked for him to pray, chant, and meditate in order to get better at aikido, and so he told his students to do likewise. The founder's was a truly mystical approach and as such a very personal one, for in order for real transmission of the knowledge to take place, the student had to possess an intuitive gift and follow practices not unlike Ueshiba's own in order make rational sense of the founder's explanations of the art. Unfortunately, the vast majority of aikido resources in the world today are still infused with these pre-rational conceptualizations of the art, and as a result, the students continue to remain confused about basic elements.

The second way that spirituality and aikido intersect is through the interpretation of the art as a form of budo, which aims not merely at the object of winning a fight, but at refining and developing

168

character. Though this budo ethic has long existed in the Japanese arts, it did not come to be the dominant idea until modern times. Early Japanese martial arts were called bujutsu and were not based on this model. To understand this divergence we must look to the difference between Do and Jutsu. The contrast between these two concepts can be made in a number of ways. For instance, the character of Jutsu is composed of the element gyo, meaning road or way, and shutsu, meaning to stick to the stem, so we have the concept of "the way that people have stuck to, the traditional way, the way something has always been done." The term Do (or michi) is compounded of shin nyu, meaning foot movement, and shu, meaning head; thus, we have the concept of "facing in the direction we want to go, implying a way of thinking or direction that one must follow to get to a destination." So fundamentally we see that Jutsu points to the past, while Do points toward the future.

Moreover, Mr. Tomiki described the difference between Jutsu and Do in that the whole focus in bujutsu was on victory in combat (these were methods developed for use by soldiers after all) and understanding the ways of victory were the sole aim of its method. In budo, however, we find a method that embraces both victory and defeat, forming a balanced picture wherein our knowledge of both outcomes are useful and positive. We learn from victory and we learn from our defeat; both are equally important and necessary, and it is only by studying both that we can ultimately transcend both victory and defeat. Following the path of Jutsu secures us victory over others; the path of Do offers a chance to be victorious over ourselves.

In aikido we are practicing a Do form, and just as in all classical budo, aikido functions not merely as a means of self-defense, but rather as a means of transforming individuals into better human beings. This transformative aspect is the spiritual essence of the art. Through diligent practice and study, we become infused with the higher values of trust, honesty, commitment, flexibility, and harmony. The practice of this art naturally allows us to evolve toward ever higher standards and fulfill our human potential.

As a spiritual way, the art of aikido need not strive to any otherworldly, supernatural goals. Aikido is not about becoming a saint or a bodhisattva, or getting magic powers, or going to heaven. Rather, this art offers a means to "physicalize," or embody through action, higher ethical principles that are based on harmony and love. Perhaps this is what Ueshiba meant when he said, "True budo is love."

By practicing constantly to bring order out of chaos, to bring harmony to conflict, to make peace where there is violence, we become somehow greater than we were. We learn to handle conflicts of all shapes, sizes, and varieties through the active use of principle. And in practicing these principles with one another, we are constantly in a state of giving and receiving, of sharing ourselves, our bodies, and minds with our partners. An active and authentic trust develops from this interaction, for we know, in no uncertain terms, how easily our partner could hurt or injure us, but time and again we trust, we give ourselves away to one another, and time and again, we are taken care of and protected from harm. The development of such a high degree of trust is rare in life; few people have the good fortune to experience it at all. But in aikido, it becomes the standard. If we train with higher principles and strive at all times to take care of one another, we will develop hundreds, if not thousands, of such trusting relationships over a lifetime of practice. Such trust is a truly spiritual bond – not on some otherworldly dimension, but in day to day reality.

This network of trust, this profound spiritual bond, affords us greater confidence and security in our lives, for no matter how crazy life may become, we have a safe haven that we can always enter. We have a stable community of trusting relationships to fall back on.

The practice of these principles also has a marked effect on communication, for as we constantly give to and receive from one another in a safe and authentic way, we learn how to share ourselves in safe and authentic ways. The practice itself shapes the practitioner's character and actions toward becoming more open, honest, and safe individuals who are capable of expressing themselves without fear or malice. Just as we practice clarity in our attacks and techniques, we come to also practice clarity in our daily lives. Just as we overcome and peel away layers of self-deception in our practice, we also shed the phony parts of ourselves that interfere with our ability to establish harmony and well being in our relationships with those around us. We learn to trust ourselves, to be our authentic selves, and to live in a state of heightened spontaneity and intuitive understanding of ourselves and others. To experience this greater clarity and live it out is an incredible spiritual gift that aikido gives to us.

Aikido is a truly spiritual path, but it need not be a religious one. It does not require belief in any god or gods and need not be practiced with rituals or any religious dogma. Spiritual Aikido has no formal indoctrination or conversion. It requires no prayer, chants, or meditation, yet it embodies and enacts such high values of ethics that it comes to purify and refine those who practice it. Whether they are aware of it or not, aikidoka become transformed; they adapt and change for the better. They are enriched and empowered by the practice toward fuller, more complete lives. On one level, this is what Ueshiba called "misogi," spiritual purification, and it is what takes us beyond the martial art as a means of destruction and killing (bujutsu), through to a means of self transformation (budo), and finally to an existence in higher spiritual values (bushin).

Bushin is not a goal, but it is a state that comes unsought for and without warning. To approach bushin, is to approach a different scale of life altogether. The sense of true openness, true emptiness, that seems so vast in scope that it contains all contradictions within its intuitive clarity, is perhaps best described as enlightenment, but even here it is not some mystical hocus pocus, but the natural by product of a refined, focused, and trained awareness in action. Such a state of being is not dependent on religious practice or ritual; you need not chant the kotodama, sit under waterfalls, or make offerings to buddha; for, it is as simple as awakening to your own true self and letting go of all plans, opinions, concepts, or designs. This is a state of mind beyond the confines of belief and dogma, existing in pure flowing awareness; existing in a state of Aiki with the universe.

171

Conclusion

In conclusion, I want to express my heartfelt gratitude to my aikido senseis. These men and women are the giants whose shoulders I've come to stand upon so as to achieve my view. I understand that the only way I might repay the tremendous debt I owe to my teachers is to try to pass on what they have given me. Indeed, I feel obliged to transmit as clearly as possible the wisdom and insight that they have shared with me so that their aikido can travel into the future through succeeding generations of students. It is in the spirit of this service toward the future of aikido that I have written this text, as one small way of paying back the great debt and obligation I have incurred through my years of training.

Next, I want to thank the beginning students of Aikido, for without you the art would fade and die. The art continues because you as students continue to be interested enough in it to want to learn and eventually pass it on yourselves.

I sincerely hope that this book will help both students and teachers of Aikido; I hope that it will make a positive difference in someone's aikido life, and that it will further the transmission of high quality Aikido into the future.

Finally, I ask that you attribute any and all flaws and faults that you find in this book solely on me and my own incomplete or eccentric understanding of this infinite art. I accept complete responsibility for the sin of overstepping my qualifications. Please lay any blame you have at my feet and not at the feet of my teachers, whose clarity and depth of understanding far exceeds my own.

Thank You
Nick Lowry

Recommended Reading and Study

1. **Book of Twelve Winds** by Karl Geis
   This is simply the best book of aikido philosophy that the author has ever read.

2. *Fugakukai Films series* of Aikido films by Karl Geis, filmed by George Webber
   The best technical resource outside of a competent instructor. Covers everything from fundamentals to higher kata. An amazing body of knowledge.

3. **Judo and Aikido** by Kenji Tomiki
   An out of print classic. The first book in English about Aikido.

4. **Book of Five Rings** by Miyamoto Musashi, translated by Thomas Cleary,
   A classical book of strategy that has influenced all Japanese martial arts since the time of its writing in 1643.

5. **Way and the Power** by F.J. Lovret
   A modern book of Japanese strategy.

6. **Sword of No-Sword** by John Stevens
   The life of the greatest Zen Swordsman of the nineteenth century.

7. **Abundant Peace** by John Stevens
   The life of Ueshiba, founder of Aikido.

8. **Tomiki Aikido** vol. 1 and 2 by Dr. Lee Ah Loi
   Helpful resources, particularly vol. 2 for higher kata.

9. **Zen and the Ways** by Trevor Legget
   Great insights and anecdotes by a true Judo man.

10. **Classical Bujutsu**, **Classical Budo**, and **Modern Budo And Bujutsu** - by Donn Draeger
Perhaps the best historical record of Japanese martial ways and arts published in English.

Appendix I : Aikido Syllabus Beginner to Blackbelt

(Note: the material in this appendix may be reproduced and distributed without the author's permission.)

The following syllabus is designed as an aid to students and teachers of aikido and is intended to be used in conjunction with **Aikido: principles of kata and randori** by Nick Lowry; illustrations and technical descriptions of each kata can be found in this text. In addition, it is recommended that students and teachers also refer to the Aikido film series from **Fugakukai Films**, available from GW Enterprises 1513 N. Washington, Enid, Oklahoma, 73701; tel. (405) 233-6912. The technical and general promotion standards listed in this syllabus are consistent with those recognized by the Fugakukai International Aikido Association under Shihan Karl Geis. Further information on promotion standards and technical requirements can be obtained from the Karl Geis web page: **http://www.karlgeis.com** or by contacting Karl Geis 1413 Butlercrest, Houston, Texas, 77808; tel. (713) 468-4879.

White Belt to Yonkyu (Total: 40 hr -- 3 months)
Safety rules and etiquette
Ukemi: back fall, side fall, break fall position, low rolling break fall
Tegatana no Kata (walking kata): blocked in and memorized
Hanasu no Kata (8 releases): blocked in and memorized -- focus on pushing
Ju Nana hon Kata (the Seventeen): Atemi waza section (1-5) blocked in and memorized
Study of Basic Principles: student will be given a basic intellectual grasp of the physical principles -- unbendable arm, ma-ai, same hand and foot, center, posture, move off line of the attack
Test Requirements for Yonkyu (green belt): the walking kata, 8 releases, 1-5 of the Seventeen

175

Yonkyu to Sankyu (Total: 80 hr -- 6 months)

Ukemi: continued study of basic ukemi, beginning standing rolling break falls

Tegatana no Kata (the walking kata): continued study and refinement -- begin to relate principles to movements

Hanasu no Kata (8 releases): continued study and refinement -- focus on following uke

Ju Nana hon Kata(the Seventeen): continued study and refinement of Atemi waza (1-5)
and Hiji waza section (6-10) blocked out and memorized

Principles: Student begins to apply the physical principles to all katas

Introduction to Randori: basic concepts and rules of hand randori and an introduction to knife randori

Introduction to survival based grappling skills

Test Requirements for Sankyu (third brown): 1-10 of the Seventeen

Sankyu to Nikyu (Total: 120 hrs. -- 9 months)

Ukemi: continued refinement of all previous skills plus dynamic rolling break falls and the beginning of elevated break falls

Tegatana no Kata (the walking kata): continued study and refinement -- beginning of internalization of principles

Hanasu no Kata (8 releases): continued study and refinement -- focus on consistent application of principles and beginning of internalization -- timing and synchronization

Ju Nana hon Kata (the Seventeen): continued study and refinement of first two sections (1-10) plus Tekubi waza section (11-14) blocked out and memorized

Principles: Student begins to internalize physical principles in all katas

Randori: continued study -- drills, emphasis on noncompetitive focus for hand randori

Test Requirements for Nikyu (second brown): 1-14 of the Seventeen

Nikyu to Ikkyu (Total: 150 hrs. -- 12 months)

Ukemi: continued study of all previous skills plus introduction to side rolling break fall, spinning rolls, accelerated rolls, and rolls without arms

Tegatana no Kata (the walking kata): continued study and refinement

Hanasu no Kata (8 releases): continued study and refinement -- introduction of flowing movement

Ju Nana hon Kata (the Seventeen): continued study and refinement of first three sections (1-14) plus Uki waza section (15-17) blocked out and memorized, beginning of internalization of Atemi waza

Principles: continued study and internalization of physical principles and introduction to strategic and conceptual principles

Randori: improvement of randori skills -- continued focus on non-competitive drills

Introduction to multiple attack training

Introduction to the rudiments of teaching

Test Requirements for Ikkyu (first brown with black sleeve): 1-17 of the Seventeen

Ikkyu to Shodan (Total: 250 hrs.-- 18 months)

Ukemi: continued study of all previous skills plus introduction to garuma break falls

Tegatana no Kata (the walking kata): continued study and refinement

Hanasu no Kata (8 releases): continued study and refinement

Ju Nana hon Kata (the Seventeen): continued study and refinement of all sections (1-17), internalization of kata progresses

Owaza Ju Pon (Big Ten): first five techniques blocked in and memorized

Principles: continued study and internalization of physical, conceptual, strategic, and tactical principles

Randori: improvement of randori skills

Test Requirements: to qualify for Shodan (first degree black belt) in Aikido the student must be able to demonstrate all of the above katas (the walk, 8 releases, the Seventeen, and 1-5 of the Big Ten) and should have a good working vocabulary of Aikido terminology.

Appendix II : Higher kata

The following kata are forms preserved from the older style aikido and are studied from the rank of Shodan and above.

Koryu-Dai-San (a.k.a. San Kata)

Suwari-waza (Kneeling Techniques)

1 .Oshi-taoshi
2. Gyaku-gamae-ate
3. Kote-gaeshi
4. Ryote-mochi-sukui-nage
5. Tentai-kote-hineri
6. Shiho-nage
7. Gedan-ate
8. Hiji-kime

Tachi-waza (Standing Techniques)

9. Kote-mawashi
10. Uchi-tenkai-nage
11. Gyaku-gamae-ate
12. Hiji-kime
13. Mae-otoshi
14. Ushiro-waza-mae-otoshi
15. Ushiro-waza-tentai-kote-hineri
16. Mune-tori-kata-gatame

Tanto-dori (Techniques against Knife)

17. Ushiro-ate
18. Gyaku-gamae-ate
19. Tentai-oshi-taoshi
20. Ushiro-ate

21. Ude-gatame
22. Kote-gaeshi
23. Tentai-kote-hineri
24. Shomen-giri-gedan-ate

Tachi-dori (Techniques against Sword)

25. Mae-otoshi
26. Shiho-nage
27. Ai-gamae-ate
28. Oshi-otoshi
29. Hiji-kujiki

Jo-no-bu Jo-dori (Techniques against Jo)

30. Gyaku-gamae-ate
31. Shomen-ate
32. Hishigi
33. Renraku-waza-hiji-hishigi
34. Irimi-mae-otoshi

Jo-no-bu Jo-no-tsukai-kata (Techniques using Jo)

35. Migi-sumi-otoshi
36. Migi-sumi-gori-hidari-sumi-otoshi
37. tekubi-kime-(gori)-shomen-tsuki
38. Mae-otoshi
39. Shiho-nage
40. Shiho-nage-gyaku-kaiten-nage
41. Ude-kujiki
42. Kokyu-nage

Tachi-tai-tachi (Sword against Sword)

43. Ai-uchi-men
44. Hidari-men

45. Migi-men
46. Tsuki
47. Do
48. Kote-nuki-kote
49. Kaeshi-men
50. Hasso-waki-gamae

Koryu-Dai-Yon

Shichihon-no-nage-no-kata (Seven forms Balance Breaking)

1. Jodan-ai-gamae
2. Jodan-gyaku-gamae
3. Chudan-ai-gamae
4. Chudan-gyaku-gamae
5. Gedan-ai-gamae
6. Gedan-gyaku-gamae
7. Ushiro-ryote-mochi

Shichihon-no-nage-no-kata Ura-waza (Balance Breaking Counters)

8. Jodan-ai-gamae
9. Jodan-gyaku-gamae
10. Chudan-ai-gamae
11. Chudan-gyaku-gamae
12. Gedan-ai-gamae
13. Gedan-gyaku-gamae
14. Ushiro-ryote-mochi

Tachi-waza (Standing Techniques)

15. Migi-gyaku-gamae-ate
16. Hidari-gyaku-gamae ate
17. Uchi-kaiten-nage
18. Sukui-nage

19. Ushiro-waza-kote-gaeshi
20. Jyuji-garami-nage
21. Tentai-oshi-taoshi
22. Tentai-hiji-garami
23. Tentai-sukui-nage
24. Ryote-mochi-uki-otoshi
25. Tenkai-kote-kujiki

Koryu-Dai-Go

Suwari-waza (Kneeling Techniques)

1. Oshi-taoshi
2. Tentai-oshi-taoshi
3. Tekubi-osae
4. Tentai-oshi-otoshi
5. Kokyu-nage
6. Kote-gaeshi
7. Sukui-nage

Tachi-waza (Standing Techniques)

8. Tenchi-nage
9. Ryote-mochi-sukui-nage
10 .Ryote-mochi-sukashi-nage
11. Ryote-mochi-shiho-nage
12. Gyaku-kote-gaeshi

Tachi-waza (Standing Techniques)

13. Hidari-gamae-men-uchi-irimi
14. Migi-gamae-men-uchi-irimi
15. Migi-gyaku-gamae-ate
16. Hidari-gyaku-gamae-ate

17. Uchi-kaiten-nage
18. Sukui-nage

Tachi-waza (Standing Techniques)

19. Yokomen-uchi-uki-otoshi
20. Yokomen-uchi-kokyu-nage
21. Yokomen-uchi-shomen-ate
22. Yokomen-uchi-sukashi-nage
23. Yokomen-uchi-hiki-otoshi

Koryu-Dai-Roku

Suwari-waza (Kneeling Techniques)

1. Oshi-taoshi
2. Tentai-oshi-taoshi
3. Hiki-taoshi
4. Tenkai-waki-gatame
5. Ryote-mochi-sumi-otoshi

Tachi-waza (Standing Techniques)

6. Hiki-otoshi
7. Mae-otoshi
8. Sukui-nage
9. Mae-otoshi
10. Sukai-koho-nage
11. Tentai-nage
12. Ushiro-tentai-nage
13. Ushiro-otoshi
14. Ushiro-nage-kote-gaeshi
15. Tentai-sukui-nage

Tachi-waza (Standing Techniques)

16 Uke-otoshi
17. Jodan-sukui-nage
18. Tentai-mae-otoshi
19. Tentai-saka-otoshi
20. Katate-mochi-irimi-nage
21. Katate-mochi-shiho-nage
22. Katate-mochi-hiji-kujiki

Tanto-dori (Techniques against Knife)

23. Irimi-nage
24. Tentai-shiho-nage
25. Tentai-ude-garami
26. Kote-mawashi
27. Koshi-garuma

Tanto-dori (Techniques using Knife)

28. Irimi-nage
29. Tentai-gyaku-gamae-ate
30. Kote-mawashi
31. Ryote-mochi-irimi-nage

Tachi-dori (Techniques against Sword)

32. Oshi-taoshi
33. Waki-gatame
34. Hineri-oshi-taoshi-nage
35. Kote-gaeshi

Jo-no-bu Jo-no-tsukai-kata (Techniques using Jo)

36. Tentai-ushiro-otoshi
37. Tentai-ashi-barai

38. Tentai-mae-otoshi
39. Kote-mawashi-ude-garami

Appendix III: A Short Biography of Kenji Tomiki

1900 born March 15 in Tsunodate in Aiki prefecture

1906 early interest in sword work

1910 begins judo training and in high school wins honors in both academics and sports

1924 enters Waseda University, joins judo club rank of shodan, begins training at the Kodokan with Kano

1925 nidan in judo

1926 sandan in judo, introduced by a classmate to Ueshiba and begins studies in aikijujitsu at Omoto headquarters in Ayabe

1927 yondan in judo, degree in political science and begins graduate school

1928 godan in judo

1929 enters the Tenranjiai Imperial Tournament, a judo competition of unprecedented scale, held to mark the emperor Hirohito's ascension. Finishes in the top 12 competitors but must withdraw due to injury

1933 plays a major role in preparing Ueshiba's training manual "Budo Renshu"

1934 recognized as one of the senior instructors at Ueshiba's Kobukan Dojo in Wakamatsu-cho

1936 Kano requests that Tomiki research aikido for possible inclusion in the judo curriculum as rikakutaisei waza (judo at a distance)

1936 Moves to Japanese occupied Manchuria to teach at Daido Gakuin

1938 accepts teaching position at Kenkoku University in Manchuria and heads aiki-budo program

1938 Kano dies, Nango named successor at the Kodokan

1940 Ueshiba grants Menkyo Kaiden (hachidan) to Tomiki, he is the first of Ueshiba's students to receive this rank. Tomiki remains on teaching staff of Hombu Dojo until 1960

1941-44 Returns periodically to Japan to work at the Kodokan with the newly formed rikakutaisei research group. Group is headed by Murakami and includes: Nagaoka, Samura, Mifune, and Iizuka. Tomiki is the primary lecturer

1944 publishes "A Systematic Study of Rikakutaisei Waza in Judo"

1945-48 Tomiki is interned in Soviet prison camp in Siberia, while a prisoner invents judo taiso

1948 Returns to Japan, works to restore the practice of Judo (all training was suspended after the war), and joins the Physical Education section at Waseda University, works as an administrator at the Kodokan

1950 made permanent manager of All Japan Judo Federation

1951 Made full time professor at Waseda University, head of the Waseda Judo Club, continues study and instruction of rikakutaisei

1952-60 develops and teaches a "practical course in judo exercises" that includes 12 kata techniques found safe for randori, Ueshiba requests that Tomiki bring his system back to the Hombu dojo but the inner group of Ueshiba's followers reject Tomiki's research. In 1960, Tomiki changes the name of his system to Aikido

1953 Tours the US teaching Judo

1954 publishes textbook " Judo Exercises"

1958 PE board at Waseda approves the establishment of Aikido Club

1956 publishes "Judo and Aikido," the first introduction of aikido in English

1964 hachi dan in judo

1968 helps to found the Japanese Martial Arts Research Society, serves as vice president until 1973

1973-79 teaches and writes extensively on martial arts

1974 founds the Japan Aikido Association

1978 diagnosed with intestinal cancer

1979 Dies on Christmas Day

Glossary

A

ai	joining together, harmony
aigame	regular facing posture
aiki	harmony of spirit or intent
aikidoka	a student of aikido
aikijujitsu	old style combat oriented art from which aikido originated
ate	to hit or strike a certain point
atemi	to hit the body
ato no sen	the moment of initiative taken in response to the attack
ashi	foot or leg
ayumi ashi	normal walking with feet alternating

B

barai	sweep
bu	martial, military
budo	study of martial arts as away of life so as to cultivate character
budoka	a student of budo, implies a great understanding of martial arts
bujutsu	tudy of martial arts as a form of practice for combat, military science
bushin	"martial spirit" transcendental level of martial arts

C

chudan	middle level, area from the hips to the shoulders
chushin	center line of the body

D

dai	prefix for numbers (i.e. dai-san, the third)

189

Daito ryu	ancient martial arts school that originated in the middle ages and was passed down by the Takeda clan
dan	a degree of rank in black belt
do	torso
do	the way, a path of refinement, practice and study
dojo	"way place" a training hall for study of the martial arts
dori	to grasp

F

Fugakukai	a martial arts association begun by Karl Geis, Tsunako Miyake, and Takeshi Inoue for the preservation and higher research of Tomiki aikido

G

gaeshi	reversal
gamae	posture or stance
garami	entanglement
garuma	wheel, in a throw, to rotate horizontally as well as vertically
gatame	lock
gedan	low position, hip level
Geis, Karl	10th dan aikido, 8th dan judo, 8th dan jodo, began aikido training in 1957 at Waseda University first under Miyake Tsunako and later Kenji Tomiki, Promoted to 6th dan by Tomiki in 1969, president of Fugakukai now known as Karl Geis Ryu
giri	cut
go	five
godan	fifth degree black belt
gokyu	fifth grade before black belt, orange belt
goshi	hip
gyaku	reverse

H

hachi	eight
hanasu	to escape, to obtain release from
Hanasu no Kata	the eight releases, related to old style shichi hon no kuzushi
hando no kuzushi	the pendulum like quality of balance and off balance
hara	abdomen
hasso	shoulder height ready position with sword
hazumi	force generated by the unified action of ones whole body movement
hidari	left
hiji	elbow
hiki	to pull
hineri	twist
hishigi	crushing
hon	main, normal, standard

I

ichi	one
ikioi	force generated by isolated muscular strength, "using muscle"
ikkyu	first grade before black belt, brown belt with black collar
irimi	entering by sliding past your opponent as in a balance break
itten	one spot, center of gravity just below the navel

J

jodan	high position, shoulder level and above
jodo	way of the short staff, a tradition weapons art
ju	ten
ju	gentleness, yielding, softness
juji (jyuji)	cross
Ju Nana Hon Kata	Seventeen standard forms, also called randori no kata

ju no ri	principle of gentleness
ju yoko go sei suru	old saying "soft controls hard"
judo	martial art derived from jujitsu by Jigoro Kano, the preeminent throwing and grappling art in the world

K

kaeshi	counter
kaiten	rotation
kake	to execute a throw
Kano, Jigoro	(1860-1938) founder of judo, a revolutionary figure in martial arts
kansetsu	joint technique
kata	formal exercise to demonstrate principles
kata	shoulder
katate	one hand
ki	spirit or life
kime	focus
Kito ryu	ancient school of martial arts that emphasized throwing and off balance
kohai	the junior grade in any pair of training partners
Kogure, Riki	8th Dan aikido, aikido pioneer who was among the first teachers in the U.S. when he spent six years in Houston, Texas at the Karl Geis School. Currently the CEO of the Japan Aikido Association
kokyu	breath
koryu kata	ancient forms preserved for advanced study
koshi	hips
kote	wrist
ku	nine
kubi	neck
kujiki	twist
kuzure no jotai	forms of off balance

kuzushi	the disruption of posture and breaking of balance
kyu	grades of rank before black belt

M

ma-ai	distance of engagement and reaction
mae	front
mae ukemi	forward fall
mawashi	to turn
men	face
metsuke	eye contact
migi	right
Miyake, Tsunako	a profound master of several martial arts including: aikido, judo, jodo, and tai chi, who was instrumental in the development of many of the katas in the Tomiki system
mizu no kokoro	mind clear and reflective like water
mochi	a grip
mugame	empty posture, no special stance, just natural
mune	chest
Musashi, Miyamoto	(1584-1645) great swordsman and martial arts genius who wrote *The Book of Five Rings*
mushin	no mind, an open readiness unencumbered by intentions or plans

N

nagashi no ri	principle of flowing
nage	throw
namba	same hand and foot movement
ni	two
ni kyu	second grade before black belt, brown belt
nidan	second degree black belt
nuki	pull

O

Osae	to immobilize
oshi	push
osu	push
otoshi	drop
Owaza Ju Pon	the big ten defensive throws

R

randori	free exercise, both partners simultaneously attacking and defending
randori no kata	old name for Ju Nana Hon Kata
renraku	continuous flow of successive techniques
ri	principle
riai	"principle harmony" underlying logic of a kata or technique
rikakutaisei	literally, techniques used when standing apart from your opponent, "judo at a distance" i.e. aikido
roku	six
rokudan	sixth degree black belt, red and white belt
rokyu	sixth grade before black belt, yellow belt
ryote	both hands
ryote-dori	grabbing both hands

S

saka	down
san	three
sandan	third degree black belt
sankyu	third grade before black belt, brown belt
sempai	senior grade in any pair of training partners
sen	the moment of initiative occurring simultaneously with the attack
sen-sen no sen	seizing the initiative just as the attack is about to begin
sensei	teacher, usually 4th dan or above

shi	four
shiai	contest
shichi	seven
shichi hon no kuzushi	early form of Hanasu no Kata
shihan	honorific title, "a leader of men," a teacher of 6th dan or above
shiho	four directions
shizen hon tai	natural upright body posture
shizen no ri	principle of natural posture
shizumi	weakness in body structure or movement
shodan	first degree black belt
shomen	front
shugyo	hard training
soto	outside
sukashi	opening
sukui	scooping
sumi	corner
suwari	seated position

T

tachi	standing
tachi	sword
tai sabaki	body movement, esp. evasion
taiso	warm up exercises
Takeda, Sokaku	(1860-1943) famous Daito ryu teacher who taught Ueshiba aikijujitsu.
tanto	knife
taoshi	to tip over
te	hand or arm
tegatana	"hand sword" unbendable arm
Tegatana no kata	the walking kata
tekubi	wrist
tenchi	heaven and earth
tenkai (tentai)	rotation, turning around
tenkai kotegaeshi	alternative name for shihonage
tenkan	to turn around and reverse direction

tobu ukemi	jumping fall, an elevated forward rolling breakfall, a flip
tokui waza	favorite technique
Tomiki, Kenji	(1900-1980) menkyo kaiden from Ueshiba, 8th dan judo, renowned scholar and researcher in the martial arts, founder of Tomiki ryu
Tomiki ryu	style of aikido emphasizing a logical curriculum and effective technical standards
tori	the person who applies the technique
toshu randori	hand randori
tsugi ashi	following step, sliding steps with same foot leading
tsuki	thrust
tsukuri	to fit in with body position

U

uchi	inside
ude	arm
Ueshiba, Morihei	(1883-1969) founder of aikido, also referred to as O Sensei by many
ue-shita	up/down, body rise and body drop
uke	the person who receives the technique
ukemi	art of falling or receiving techniques in a safe and efficient manner
uki	floating
unsoku	footwork
ura	behind
ushiro	rear
ushiro ukemi	back falls

W

waki	side of the body
waza	technique

Y

yoko	side
yoko ukemi	side fall
yondan	fourth degree black belt
yonkyu	fourth grade before black belt, green belt

Z

zanshin	state of ready awareness; without concept or distraction
zempo kaiten ukemi	forward rolling break fall

Order Form

Additional copies of this book,
Aikido, Principles of Kata and Randori by Nick Lowry,
a **Book of Twelve Winds** by Karl Geis,
and the **Fugakukai Films**
(a full technical series of aikido Video tapes by Karl Geis)
are available from GW Enterprises

Postal Orders:
GW Enterprises
1513 N. Washington
Enid, Oklahoma, 73701

Telephone orders: (580) 233-6912.

Name:
Address:
City: **State:**
Zip:
tel: (   )

**Send today for the current catalog and prices
and for further information on books and tapes see
the Karl Geis website at**

www. karlgeis.com

Printed in July 2019
by Rotomail Italia S.p.A., Vignate (MI) - Italy